I0153017

IN THE ORDER
OF MELCHIZEDEK

IN THE ORDER
OF MELCHIZEDEK

The Truth about Tithing in the New Testament

EMEKA JUDE ICHEKU

RESOURCE *Publications* · Eugene, Oregon

IN THE ORDER OF MELCHIZEDEK
The Truth about Tithing in the New Testament

Copyright © 2022 Emeka Jude Icheku. All rights reserved. Except for brief
quotations in critical publications or reviews, no part of this book may
be reproduced in any manner without prior written permission from the
publisher. Write: Permissions, Wipf and Stock Publishers, 199 W. 8th Ave.,
Suite 3, Eugene, OR 97401.

Resource Publications
An Imprint of Wipf and Stock Publishers
199 W. 8th Ave., Suite 3
Eugene, OR 97401

www.wipfandstock.com

PAPERBACK ISBN: 978-1-6667-9331-4
HARDCOVER ISBN: 978-1-6667-9330-7
EBOOK ISBN: 978-1-6667-9332-1

JANUARY 7, 2022 11:23 AM

Scripture taken from the New King James Version® Copyright© 2005 by
Thomas Nelson. Used by permission. All rights reserved.

To all that seek the truth. That they may know the truth and the truth may make them free.

And to all that wrest the scriptures. That they may turn from there wicked ways.

Therefore, since we have this ministry, as we have received mercy, we do not lose heart. But we have renounced the hidden things of shame, not walking in craftiness nor handling the word of God deceitfully, but by manifestation of the truth commending ourselves to every man's conscience in the sight of God.

(2 COR 4:1, 2)

And you shall know the truth, and the truth shall make you free.

(JOHN 8:32)

Stand fast therefore in the liberty by which Christ has made us free, and do not be entangled again with a yoke of bondage.

(GAL 5:1)

Contents

THE CONTROVERSIES

A LOT OF CONTROVERSIES have been whipped up about the practice of tithing in the Church. A number of seemingly conflicting positions have been canvassed in the debate on the issue. This book is a response to a number of probing questions by some believers I have had the privilege to know in recent times. First, I was once confronted by a student of mine with questions about the scriptural correctness of tithing in the New Testament dispensation. He had been discussing the subject with a fellow student, and they, feeling that I should know better, decided to ask me for clarification.

They argued that tithing was not an issue of concern in the New Testament Church but that it related to Old Testament only. One of them asserted that though he "paid" tithe, he did so only because it was an official doctrine of his church, and not because he can defend it based on the written Word. The conversation that ensued between them and myself gave me ample reasons to be concerned and to think more deeply on the subject.

Second, I happened to be in a church worship during which a guest minister preached. For a greater part of more than an hour he preached, he was all about "tithe belongs to the man of God." He distinguished between offerings which according to him belonged to the church, and the tithe which he claimed was an exclusive entitlement of the "man of God." He further stated, among other things, that he had instructed all pastors under him to collect tithe on his behalf. Listening to this minister was very thought-provoking.

Third, I met someone who happened to be in possession of the booklet titled "The Right Way to Tithe" by Bishop Renato Cardoso. Our conversation on the subject revealed a lack of most basic critical study of the scriptures on her part. I saw in this person a Christian who had a very lopsided opinion of God as to believe that "one is cursed if one did not pay tithe to God." I realized that this person represented many of the Christians who have swallowed the "bait" of tithing, "hook, line and sinker" without trying to find for themselves what the Bible says on the subject by comparing scripture to scripture as the Berea church would have done (Acts 17:11). Such Christians live in perpetual fear, trembling before God because of an issue that God does not hold them accountable for.

In essence, there are two broad views on the debate on the scriptural correctness or otherwise of tithing in the New Testament. The first denies that tithing has a place in the New Testament. It argues that tithing was relevant to the office of the priests and Levites who were under instruction to receive tithes for the work of the house of God which they did. Proponents of this view also argue that Christ did not approve of tithing neither did the early church practice it. Therefore, it should not be accepted in contemporary church.

The second view proposes that tithing in the New Testament is a continuation of the pre-law regime of tithing as exemplified in Abraham tithing to Melchizedek. This view argues that tithing pre-dated the law, was prescribed in the law as a confirmation and preached by Christ. Therefore, it should be practiced by the contemporary church.

The aim of this book is not to dissuade Christians from bringing tithes into the house of God. Rather, its primary objective is to provide a nuanced perspective and explore a third view or a third way. This view agrees with the position that tithing is not binding or compulsory in the New Testament. However, it argues that tithing is acceptable in the church if it meets the conditions of free will choice, corporate agreement, and Spirit's leading which are pillars of New Testament worship and service to God. Furthermore, it seeks to correct some unscriptural teachings that have developed around the issue of tithing and to liberate Christians from the ungodly fear of a "lurking devourer," which fear has been instigated by some contemporary preachers.

I decided to use the booklet by Bishop Cardoso mentioned above as the basis for a critique of the doctrine and practice of tithing because it seemed to present a consensus of doctrinal perspectives among the advocates for tithing. Reference will also be made of the book titled "The Revelation of Financial Renewal" by Clive Pick. In this book, Pick fell into some of the errors of exegeses that Cardoso is guilty of. Cardoso erred in conflating firstfruits for tithes, insisting on tithing everything including child support benefits, not distinguishing between different types of tithes, claims that tithe was part of Abrahamic covenant, and mistaking Christ's rebuke of the scribes and Pharisees as approval of tithe in the New Testament.

In writing this book, I have avoided citing many human authorities. Human authorities are liable to incorrectness, misinterpretation of scriptures, either intentionally or unintentionally. In trying to educate myself further on the subject of tithing, I found an absurd level of misinterpretation and misrepresentation of the scriptures by both proponents and opponents of the subject. There were concerted efforts by both camps to uphold their positions, even if it meant wresting the scriptures. This should not be the case among Christians. Christians should correct one another in love and in humility, knowing that "he that saves a soul is wise." Thus in writing this book, I just set out to place before the reader what I read from the scriptures and not to be entangled in the contention among advocates and challengers of the subject.

However, a few exceptions were made to this decision not to cite human authorities. Where inevitable, it was necessary to cite some authorities in order to put issues in a proper perspective. Where this was done, I endeavored to cite a near-neutral and unbiased commentator. All other references regarding the biblical correctness or otherwise of the subject of this book were taken from the Bible (New King James Version).

There is a copious quotation of the scriptures in this book. This is informed, first by the fact that as Christians, the Bible is the foundation and basis of everything we believe and practice. There must be enough scriptural evidence to support what should form part of Christian doctrines especially contentious issues such as tithing.

Second, it was appropriate to quote vastly in order to make for easy reading. Considering that some people may find it a little cumbersome to turn from book to Bible whenever they need to check up a reference in the Bible, it was thought expedient to add the scriptures rather than just the references. However, in so doing, I was careful to provide a background to every Bible event or issue that needed clarification. For example, in order to give the right interpretations, relevant scriptures were not quoted in isolation of preceding or following Bible verses. In any case, reading this book with your Bible beside you will be more enriching as you will be prompted to consult your Bible further than is presented in this book.

I pray that as you read this book with an openness of heart and an attitude that seeks the truth irrespective of whether the truth kicks against your long-held views and beliefs, that the Lord whom you wish to serve in all sincerity will guide you into all truth.

ACKNOWLEDGEMENTS

I THANK THE LORD for using me as an instrument to deliver this corrective teaching in a book. It is a great privilege. I pray that his will and purpose for this book be fulfilled in all the earth.

I most certainly thank Zee, my most loving and beautiful wife. Her invaluable support and encouragement contributed immensely to bringing this book to fruition.

I am also indebted to the very warm and gracious Professor Ilana van Wyk of Stellenbosch University. Her prompt and kind assistance with very important information made a critical segment of this book possible.

I must also acknowledge my students who dragged me into their debate on the subject matter of this book, and all believers on both sides of the debate who one way or another contributed to this debate. Their arguments for or against, compelled me to write this book.

Chapter 1

THE CONCEPT

LET US START BY defining the subject of our concern: tithe. Concisely, tithe is defined as "the tenth part of the increase arising from the profits of land and stock, allotted to the clergy for their support or devoted to religious or charitable uses."[1]

The practice of tithing dated back to unknown antiquity and at least 430 years before the law of Moses.[2] The first mention of tithe in the scriptures was in Genesis 14:18–20:

> Then Melchizedek King of Salem brought out bread and wine; he was the priest of God Most High. And he blessed him and said: "Blessed be Abram of God Most High, Possessor of heaven and earth; And blessed be God Most High, Who has delivered your enemies into your hand." And he gave him a tithe of all.

The second mention of tithe was in Genesis 28:20–22 where Jacob made a vow to God that he would give a tithe to Him:

> Then Jacob made a vow, saying, "If God will be with me, and keep me in this way that I am going, and give me bread to eat and clothing to put on, so that I come back to my father's house in peace, then the lord shall be my God. And this stone which I have set as a pillar shall be

1. Fanning, *Tithes*

2. Dake, *Annotated Reference Bible*

God's house, and of all that You give me I will surely give a tenth to You."

Tithing was incorporated into the law of Moses as a statutory basis for the Jewish welfare system. This welfare system was part and parcel of the Jewish theocratic system. In Leviticus 27:30, 32 the Lord commanded that "all the tithe of the land, whether of the seed of the land or of the fruit of the tree, is the LORD's. It is holy to the LORD. And concerning the tithe of the herd or the flock, of whatever passes under the rod, the tenth one shall be holy to the LORD."

Thus, in the Old Testament, believers set aside a tenth of their agricultural yields for religious purposes, that is, support for the clergy, and charitable uses which encompassed their welfare system and indeed other specific aspects of their lives. The various purposes of tithe were reflected in the different types of tithes that obtained in the Old Testament.

TYPES OF TITHES

Under the Old Testament law, there were five types of tithes. Four were commanded by God. The fifth type of tithe was an imposition by man. The first three kinds of tithes were annual and regular tithes while the fourth type was a tri-annual tithe. These four types of tithes were commanded in order to support people who (for reasons such as their call) are to minister on the altar of God, such as the Levites and priests, and those who became destitute or poor as a result of their social and material conditions such as widows, orphans, and strangers. The following are the types of tithes recorded in the scriptures:

The Prerogative (Levitical) Tithe

The first type of tithe was meant for the Levites and priests alone. This was to cater for the Levites and the institution of the priesthood which God commanded Moses to establish. Thus the tithe which the people of Israel paid to the Lord, he gave the Levites which included the priests:

> Then the Lord said to Aaron: "You shall have no in-
> heritance in their land, nor shall you have any portion
> among them; I am your portion and inheritance among
> the children of Israel. Behold, I have given the children
> of Levi all the tithes in Israel as an inheritance in return
> for the work they perform, the work of the tabernacle of
> meeting. For the tithes of the children of Israel, which
> they offer up as a heave offering to the LORD, I have
> given to the Levites as an inheritance; therefore I have
> said to them, 'Among the children of Israel they shall
> have no inheritance'" (Num 18:20, 21, 24).

The Levites and the priests of the Old Testament (of which Aaron was the first) were forbidden from having a share of the inheritance in the land of Israel, according to God's commandment: "You shall have no inheritance in their land, nor shall you have any portion among them." That meant that they were not allowed to participate in any form of income yielding activity such as farming. They were to be dedicated to the work of the tabernacle of the Lord. Therefore, when the Promised Land was divided, it was divided among the other eleven tribes excluding the Levites. Thus, the other eleven tribes of Israel got portions except the tribe of Levi. To compensate the Levites and the priests, God commanded that tithes from the eleven tribes be paid to the Levites "in return for the work they perform, the work of the tabernacle of meeting." From this point onward, tithing became a commandment. It was no longer optional and no one was to question it during the Old Testament. It was to be obeyed. So God commanded the children of Israel to pay tithes to the Levites and the priests because of their peculiar circumstances as ministers of God's tabernacle. Thus, in the Old Testament, people brought a tenth of their yields whether of farm produce or animals to the Levites. This was done to support the priests, and the Levites that worked with them in the service of the altar. It was the prerogative of the Levites and priests. It was a regular tithe, which was paid as often as the children of Israel reaped their harvests. This is the kind of tithe that is well known and popularly adopted and practiced in most denominations of Christendom, with money replacing agricultural produce.

The Priestly (Aaronic) Tithe

The second type of tithe was paid to the priests by the Levites. The Levites were required to bring a tenth of the tithes they collected from the people into the storerooms in the house of God. The people were to:

> bring the firstfruits of our dough, our offerings, the fruit from all kinds of trees, the new wine and oil, to the priests, to the storerooms of the house of our God; and to bring the tithes of our land to the Levites, for the Levites should receive the tithes in all our farming communities. And the priest, the descendant of Aaron, shall be with the Levites when the Levites receive the tithes; and the Levites shall bring up a tenth of the tithes to the house of our God, to the rooms of the storehouse (Neh 10:37–38).

The firstfruits belonged to the priests while the tithes were received by the Levites. In addition to the firstfruits, the priests were also entitled to a tithe of the Levitical tithes. The people brought their tithes to the Levites, who in turn sent a tenth of the tithes to the storerooms which were for the priests. The storerooms were in the house of God, and accessible to only the priests.

The Participatory (Personal) Tithe

The third type of tithe was to be used by the person who brought it. In Deuteronomy 14:22–26, the Lord commanded:

> You shall truly tithe all the increase of your grain that the field produces year by year. And you shall eat before the LORD your God, in the place where He chooses to make His name abide, the tithe of your grain and your new wine and your oil, of the firstborn of your herds and your flocks, that you may learn to fear the LORD your God

always. But if the journey is too long for you, so that you are not able to carry the tithe, or if the place where the LORD your God chooses to put His name is too far from you, when the LORD your God has blessed you, then you shall exchange it for money, take the money in your hand, and go to the place which the LORD your God chooses. And you shall spend that money for whatever your heart desires: for oxen or sheep, for wine or similar drink, for whatever your heart desires; you shall eat there before the LORD your God, and you shall rejoice, you and your household.

The Bible records that "Now the whole congregation of the children of Israel assembled together at Shiloh, and set up the tabernacle of meeting there. And the land was subdued before them" (Josh 18:1). From this time, the children of Israel were supposed to go up to Shiloh to worship and rejoice before the Lord yearly. For example, Elkanah, the father of Samuel the man of God went up to Shiloh every year (1 Sam 1:1–3). To cater for this solemn festival at Shiloh, each person or household was required to take a tithe of the increase of the grain of their field and use such tithe for the festival. For everybody to take part in this solemn occasion, the Lord commanded that those who lived far from Shiloh should convert this tithe to money and take the money to Shiloh where they were expected to spend the money on anything that their hearts desired. This is a type of tithe that most people in the church do not know about.

The Philanthropy (The Poor) Tithe

The fourth type of tithe called "tithe for the poor"[3] was meant to provide for not only the Levites but also the orphans, widows and strangers in Israel. The Lord commanded that:

> At the end of every third year you shall bring out the tithe of your produce of that year and store it up within your gates. And the Levites, because he has no portion

3. Weisberg, *Jewish Perspective*, 20.

nor inheritance with you, and the stranger and the fatherless and the widow who are within your gates, may come and eat and be satisfied, that the LORD your God may bless you in all the work of your hands which you do (Deut 14:28–29).

God re-emphasized this command in Deuteronomy 26:12–13:

When you have finished laying aside all the tithe of your increase in the third year – the year of tithing – and have given it to the Levite, the stranger, the fatherless, and the widow, so that they may eat within your gates and be filled, then you shall say before the LORD your God: I have removed the holy tithe from my house, and also have given them to the Levite, the stranger, the fatherless, and the widow, according to all Your commandments which You have commanded me; I have not transgressed Your commandments, nor have I forgotten them.

This tithe was a special tithe paid every third year to relieve the sufferings of the poor in the land. It was not taken to the place of worship, as the first two tithes, but distributed locally as needed throughout the three years it covered.[4] Nobody talks about this type of tithe in the contemporary church.

The fifth type of tithe was not commanded by God as it was neither a religious nor welfare requirement for the Jewish society, but Prophet Samuel's repudiation of the people's demand for a non-theocratic political order. I refer to this as the princely tithe.

The Princely (Political) Tithe

The princely tithe was an imposition by kings of Israel. The children of Israel had demanded a secular king instead of the prevailing theocracy. The Prophet Samuel laid out before the people what would be the ways and manners of the king they were demanding. He told them:

4. Dake, *Annotated Reference Bible.*

This will be the behavior of the king who will reign over you: He will take your sons and appoint them for his own chariots and to be his horsemen, and some will run before his chariots. He will appoint captains over his thousands and captains over his fifties, will set some to plow his ground and reap his harvest, and some to make his weapons of war and equipment for his chariots. He will take your daughters to be perfumers, cooks, and bakers. And he will take the best of your fields, your vineyards, and your olive groves, and give them to his servants (1 Sam 8:11–14).

When you think that the king would be satisfied with what he has taken already, he ups it by taking tithes from the people. Samuel further clarified:

He will take a tenth of your grain and your vintage, and give it to his officers and servants. And he will take your male servants, your female servants, your finest young men, and your donkeys, and put them to his work. He will take a tenth of your sheep. And you will be his servants (1 Sam 8: 15–17).

One very important point to make from the scriptures in Deuteronomy 14:22–26 quoted above is that tithes were supposed to be of agricultural produce both of plants and animals. Money (gold, silver, or any other form of money) was never commanded to be used. Money was only used in respect of participatory (personal) tithe as a temporary bearer of the value of the agricultural produce. If the place of worship where the tithe was to be used happened to be far, then the tithe was to be converted to money which was taken to the venue of worship and then re-converted to agricultural items by using the money to buy those things that were required.

Chapter 2

THE CONFUSION

IN THIS CHAPTER, A not-too-elaborate critique of Bishop Cardoso's and Clive Pick's work will be done to set the background for the position that will be taken in this book. First, Cardoso's or Pick's position will be stated, followed by a simple presentation of scriptural evidence in support of their positions, or to refute them. The following are the common misconceptions about tithing in contemporary church:

MISCONCEPTION

Tithing was an ancient practice, which has been kept and should be kept by all God-fearing people.[1]

According to Cardoso:

> Tithe is a very ancient practice kept by God fearing people everywhere. God Himself established the principle of tithing teaching it through the patriarchs, kings of Israel, the prophets and the Lord Jesus Himself.[2]

---

1. Cardoso, *Right Way*, 6.
2. Cardoso, *Right Way*, 6

Scriptural Position

That tithing was an ancient practice did not make it applicable to all eras and dispensations. God established the prerogative (Levitical) and the priestly tithes to cater for the Levites and the office of the priest. These tithes were meant only for the priests and the Levites because of their unique condition which was that they should not, and did not have an inheritance as other tribes of the children of Israel did:

> The priests, the Levites—all the tribe of Levi—shall have no part nor inheritance with Israel; they shall eat the offerings of the LORD made by fire, and His portion. Therefore they shall have no inheritance among their brethren; the LORD is their inheritance, as He said to them. And this shall be the priest's due from the people, from those who offer a sacrifice, whether it is bull or sheep: they shall give to the priest the shoulder, the cheeks, and the stomach. The firstfruits of your grain and your new wine and your oil, and the first of the fleece of your sheep, you shall give him. For the LORD your God has chosen him out of all your tribes to stand to minister in the name of the LORD, him and his sons forever (Deut 18:1–5).

The ancient practice of tithing was related to the office of a priest and king. Abraham gave a tithe to Melchizedek because he was a priest. There is no record in the Bible that Abraham, Isaac, Jacob, or the patriarchs gave a tithe to any other person than the priests.

MISCONCEPTION

Tithe was part of Abrahamic Covenant.[3]

Scriptural Position

That tithing is part of Abrahamic covenant has become the most
potent argument used by the proponents of tithing to hold their
congregations spellbound. Now, this is what the Bible says about
Abrahamic covenant:

> When Abram was ninety-nine years old, the LORD ap-
> peared to Abram and said to him, "I am Almighty God;
> walk before Me and be blameless. And I will make My
> covenant between Me and you, and will multiply you ex-
> ceedingly." Then Abram fell on his face, and God talked
> with him, saying: "As for Me, behold, My covenant is
> with you, and you shall be a father of many nations. No
> longer shall your name be called Abram, but your name
> shall be Abraham; for I have made you a father of many
> nations. I will make you exceedingly fruitful; and I make
> nations of you, and kings shall come from you. And I will
> establish My covenant between Me and you and your
> descendants after you in their generations, for an ever-
> lasting covenant, to be God to you and your descendants
> after you. Also I give to you and your descendants after
> you the land in which you are a stranger, all the land of
> Canaan, as an everlasting possession; and I will be their
> God." And God said to Abraham: "As for you, you shall
> keep My covenant, you and your descendants after you
> throughout their generations. This is My covenant which
> you shall keep, between Me and you and your descen-
> dants after you: Every male child among you shall be
> circumcised; and you shall be circumcised in the flesh
> of your foreskins, and it shall be a sign of the covenant
> between Me and you. He who is eight days old among
> you shall be circumcised, every male child in your gen-
> erations, he who is born in your house or bought with
> money from any foreigner who is not your descendant.

3. Pick, *Revelation*, 70

He who is born in your house and he who is bought with your money must be circumcised, and My covenant shall be in your flesh for an everlasting covenant. And the uncircumcised male child, who is not circumcised in the flesh of his foreskin, that person shall be cut off from his people; he has broken My covenant" (Gen 17:1–14).

This was a reaffirmation of the promise that God had given to Abraham in Genesis 15:18. The scripture records that:

On that day the LORD made a covenant with Abram, saying: "To your descendants I have given this land, from the river of Egypt to the great river, the River Euphrates."

The scriptures above contain declarations, pronouncements, promises, commandments, and instructions. Altogether they set out the covenant that God instituted between himself and Abraham. The seal of this covenant was to be engraved on the foreskin of Abraham and every male member of his household in all their generations. God viewed this covenant with much seriousness that he warned that Abraham or his household can only neglect to circumcise at the risk of being cut off which is a more serious condition than death. To be "cut off" is worse than the termination of earthly life. It is what Jesus referred to as destroying soul and body in hell (Matt 10:28). In none of these instructions did God directly or indirectly mention tithing; not even remotely. Tithe was not as serious as circumcision. The seriousness with which the children of Israel viewed circumcision led some of the disciples of Jesus Christ to try to enforce it in the New Testament. This attempt was resisted and the matter put to rest by the council in Jerusalem.

The council in Jerusalem set aside the prescriptions of the law because they understood that the believers' inheritance in God is by faith in the promises of God. After all, "if the inheritance is of the law, then it is no longer of promise" (Gal 3:18). God gave the inheritance to Abraham by promise and Abraham received it, not by fulfilling the law but as a promise from God. And "Though it is only a man's covenant, yet if it is confirmed, no one annuls or adds to it" (Gal 3:15). How much less should one annul or add to a covenant instituted by God? Abrahamic covenant neither has been annulled nor tithing added to it. Thus, linking tithe to Abrahamic covenant would amount to deliberate or inadvertent wresting or misapplication of the scriptures.

MISCONCEPTION

Tithe is synonymous with the firstfruits mentioned in the book of Revelations[4].

> It is interesting to note that the last time the Bible makes reference to the tithe is exactly in the last book, in Revelation 14:4, when it refers to the redeemed as the 'firstfruits to God and to the Lamb.[5]

Scriptural Position

Tithe is not the firstfruits, and firstfruits are not the tithe. Nehemiah 10:35–37 says:

> And we made ordinances to bring the firstfruits of our ground and the firstfruits of all fruit of all trees, year by year, to the house of the LORD; to bring the firstborn of our sons and our cattle, as it is written in the Law, and the firstborn of our herds and our flocks, to the house of our God, to the priests who minister in the house of our God; to bring the firstfruits of our dough, our offerings, the fruit from all kinds of trees, the new wine and oil, to the priests, to the storerooms of the house of our God; and to bring the tithes of our land to the Levites, for the Levites should receive the tithes in all our farming communities.

If firstfruits are tithes, they would not have brought both firstfruits and tithes because that would have amounted to double tithing. A cursory look at the Bible reveals what the firstfruits are,

4. Cardoso, *Right Way*, 6.
5. Cardoso, *Right Way*, 6.

and the use to which they were put. In Exodus 23:14–16, the Lord commanded:

> Three times you shall keep a feast to Me in the year. You shall keep the Feast of Unleavened Bread (you shall eat unleavened bread seven days, as I commanded you, at the time appointed in the month of Abib, for in it you came out Egypt; none shall appear before me empty); and the feast of Harvest, the firstfruits of your labors which you have sown in the field; and the feast of Ingathering at the end of the year, when you have gathered in the fruit of your labor from the field.

In Leviticus 23:10–11, God commanded Moses:

> Speak to the children of Israel, and say to them: 'When you come into the land which I give to you, and reap its harvest, then you shall bring a sheaf of the firstfruits of your harvest to the priest. He shall wave the sheaf before the LORD, to be accepted on your behalf; on the day after the Sabbath the priest shall wave it'.

The firstfruit is the first or early batch of crops to ripen. This is the beginning or first of harvests. The later harvest comes towards the end of the harvest or farming season. When the early fruits are harvested, a sheaf or bundle is brought to the priest for a wave offering. It is a bundle or sheaf, not a tenth part. This early harvest is celebrated by the gathering of the children of Israel as God commanded and it is called the Feast of Harvest or the Feast of Firstfruits.

In Exodus 13:1, 2, 10–16, it is written:

> Then the LORD spoke to Moses, saying, "Consecrate to Me all the firstborn, whatever opens the womb among the children of Israel, both man and beast; it is mine." You shall therefore keep this ordinance in its season from year to year. And it shall be, when the LORD brings you into the land of the Canaanites, as He swore to you and your fathers, and gives it to you, that you set apart to the LORD all that open the womb, that is, every firstborn that comes from an animal which you have; the males

shall be the LORD's. But every firstborn of a donkey you shall redeem with a lamb; and if you will not redeem it, then you shall break its neck. And all the firstborn of man among your sons you shall redeem. So it shall be, when your son asks you in time to come, saying, What is this? that you say to him, 'By strength of hand the LORD brought us out of Egypt, out of the house of bondage. And it came to pass, when Pharaoh was stubborn about letting us go, that the LORD killed all the firstborn in the land of Egypt, both the firstborn of man and the firstborn of beast. Therefore I sacrifice to the LORD all males that open the womb, but all the firstborn of my sons I redeem.' It shall be as a sign on your hand and as frontlets between your eyes, for by strength of hand the LORD brought us out of Egypt.

This commandment is further reiterated in Deuteronomy 26: 1–11:

And it shall be, when you come into the land which the LORD your God is giving you as an inheritance, and you possess it and dwell in it, that you shall take some of the first of all the produce of the ground, which you shall bring from your land that the LORD your God is giving you, and put it in a basket and go to the place where the LORD your God chooses to make His name abide. And you shall go to the one who is priest in those days, and say to him, 'I declare today to the LORD your God that I have come to the country which the LORD swore to our fathers to give us.' Then the priest shall take the basket out of your hand and set it down before the altar of the LORD your God. And you shall answer and say before the LORD your God: My father was a Syrian, about to perish, and he went down to Egypt and dwelt there, few in number, and there he became a nation, great and mighty, and populous. But the Egyptians mistreated us, afflicted us, and laid hard bondage on us. Then we cried out to the LORD God of our fathers, and the LORD heard our voice and looked on our affliction and our labor and our oppression. So the LORD brought us out of Egypt with a mighty hand and with an outstretched arm, with great

terror and with signs and wonders. He has brought us
to this place and has given us this land, a land flowing
with milk and honey; and now behold, I have brought
the firstfruits of the land which you, O LORD, have given
me.' Then you shall set it before the LORD your God,
and worship before the LORD your God. So you shall
rejoice in every good thing which the LORD your God
has given to you and your house, you and the Levite and
the stranger who is among you.

The firstfruits feast was commanded by God to commemo-
rate the great deliverance which God performed in Egypt when
he killed the firstborn of both humans and animals in Egypt, to
force Pharaoh to release the children of Israel. By this redemptive
act, God laid claim to all "firsts," whether firstfruits, firstborns of
animals, or firstborn males of the children of Israel.

The quantity of the firstfruit is the same for everyone: one
sheaf. Whether you harvested a ton or a hundred tons, you are
required to bring a sheaf. This is different from tithe which is the
tenth part of whatever one reaped. That means that if one harvested ten (10) tons, one is required to pay a tithe or tenth part or
one (1) ton, and if one harvested a hundred tons, one is required
to pay a tithe or one-tenth or ten (10) tons. Therefore, the firstfruit
and the tithe are two different things.

The firstfruit also involved the offspring of the children of Israel. Every male child that opened the womb is a firstfruit unto the
Lord. Isaac for example was a firstfruit. When Abraham wanted to
sacrifice him to God as he commanded, God substituted a lamb
for Isaac, leaving an example for the children of Israel even before
the law (Gen 22:1–14). This is different from tithe which Abraham gave to Melchizedek. Likewise, the first offspring to open the
womb of an animal is a firstfruit to the Lord. Human beings and
donkeys were redeemed by exchanging a lamb for them. Tithes
never involved humans and were never redeemable. Bringing in
the firstfruits is a thanksgiving to God. "They were used for the

great feasts of Israel so that everyone could share of the goodness of the Lord together."[6]

To categorize the believers who are the firstfruits to God and the Lamb as tithe is erroneous. That will be tantamount to saying that those believers are a tenth part of the whole population of believers that would be saved. In other words, God has fixed the number of people that should be saved, which could be calculated from the number of the tithe. No one except God knows the number of people that are, or would be saved because the promise to Abraham is that his children would be like the stars of heaven for number (Gen 15:5).

The firstfruits of the redeemed of Revelation 14:4 refers to the first batch of the great tribulation elects. Reading from verses 1 and 4:

> Then I looked, and behold, a Lamb standing on Mount Zion, and with Him one hundred and forty-four thousand, having His Father's name written on their foreheads.
> These are the ones who were not defiled with women, for they are virgins. These are the ones who follow the Lamb wherever He goes. These were redeemed from among men, being firstfruits to God and to the Lamb.

The number is a hundred and forty-four thousand, a specific number. These are children of Israel that would be saved from the great tribulation. This is a specific number, a bundle, or a bunch of elects harvested from the earth. Revelation 7:1–8 shows the distribution according to twelve tribes of Israel. These are the firstfruits or the first harvest.

After the first harvest, there will be another harvest, which is the last harvest of the righteous from the earth. Read further in verses nine to 15 of Revelation chapter 7:

> After these things I looked, and behold, a great multitude which no one could number, of all nations, tribes, peoples, and tongues, standing before the throne and before the Lamb, clothed with white robes, with palm branches

6. Dake, *Annotated Reference Bible*, 225.

in their hands, and crying out with a loud voice, saying, Salvation belongs to our God who sits on the throne, and to the Lamb! All the angels stood around the throne and the elders and the four living creatures, and fell on their faces before the throne and worshiped God, Saying: "Amen! Blessing and glory and wisdom, Thanksgiving and honor and power and might, Be to our God forever and ever. Amen" Then one of the elders answered, saying to me, "Who are these arrayed in white robes, and where did they come from?" And I said to him, "Sir, you know." So he said to me, "these are the ones who come out of the great tribulation, and washed their robes and made them white in the blood of the Lamb. Therefore they are before the throne of God, and serve Him day and night in His temple. And He who sits on the throne will dwell among them.

Verses 14 and 16 of Revelation chapter 14, say that the Lord will reap them from the earth:

Then I looked, and behold, a white cloud, and on the cloud sat One like the Son of Man, having on His head a golden crown, and in his hand a sharp sickle. So He who sat on the cloud thrust in His sickle on the earth, and the earth was reaped.

These separate harvests are symbolically represented in the Old Testament by the firstfruits and the end of the year harvests, which were celebrated in feast of the harvest and the Feast of In-gathering. The firstfruits are a specific number (in the case of Revelation, is 144,000) irrespective of the size of the harvest. Christ is the firstfruit of all that will rise from the dead, not a tithe. He is a gift, not a payment. God gave him for our redemption just as he gave Abraham a lamb in the place of Isaac.

Then after these two harvests, comes the harvest of the chaffs, the unworthy, the wicked, the unrepentant, and damned. In Revelation 14:17–20:

Then another angel came out of the temple which is in heaven, he also having a sharp sickle.And another angel came out from the altar, who had power over fire, and he cried with a loud cry to him who had the sharp sickle, saying, "Thrust in your sharp sickle and gather the clusters of the vine of the earth, for her grapes are fully ripe." So the angel thrust his sickle into the earth and gathered the vine of the earth, and threw it into the great winepress of the wrath of God.

These will be gathered and cast into the winepress of the wrath of God. Revelation chapters eight and nine, reveal the nature of this wrath.

The firstfruits of the redeemed as we can see from the scriptures above are not tithes. Likewise, the Old Testament firstfruits were not tithes. To claim otherwise would be wresting the scriptures, especially, if they are lifted and quoted out of context. It is, putting it mildly, a misinterpretation and misrepresentation of the word of God.

MISCONCEPTION

Tithe represents Jesus Christ.[7]

> The tithe represents God's own firstborn, Jesus Christ, the Son of the Most High, who was given by God to mankind, to redeem us to Himself.[8]

Scriptural Position

From the quotation above, three propositions can be derived, namely:

1. That tithe represents Christ, or that Christ is symbolized by tithe.

2. That tithe was given by God to mankind, or that God paid tithe to mankind.

7. Cardoso, *Right Way*, 6.
8. Cardoso, *Right Way*, 6.

3. That tithe was given to redeem us, or that God paid a tithe to redeem mankind.

It is very erroneous to claim that Christ is represented by tithe. If we accept that Christ was a kind of tithe, then we must be able to state who paid the tithe and to whom. If God paid Christ as a tithe, then he must have paid to someone superior because the scripture says that tithes are paid by the lesser individual to someone superior (Heb 7:7). If Christ was a tithe given to mankind, then God must have paid the tithe to mankind. In that case, mankind is superior to God and not the other way round. Again, a tithe is an obligation that is fulfilled as often as one reaped from one's husbandry. In this sense, God keeps paying tithes to mankind and the sacrifice for redemption would not have been once and for all. Tithe was never paid for the redemption of man; otherwise, it would have been paid only once. The Bible says that Christ offered himself once and for all. He is not a tithe either in reality or symbolically. Rather, he is a firstfruit.

As a firstfruit, Christ is the firstborn that was given for our redemption. He is also the firstfruit from the dead, that is, the first to resurrect from the dead, and that was once and for all. Firstfruits of humans and animals were brought to God once and for all. Once the firstborn of a woman or an animal is given to God, that woman or animal was not required to bring another firstfruit no matter how many children they had subsequently. Likewise, the firstfruit of each year's harvest was brought once a year when a bundle of the harvest was brought to the priest. This remains one sheaf irrespective of the quantity of harvest and the number of times that harvest was made from that tree or field in that farming season. Christ was given and sacrificed once and for all. He is not sacrificed time and again as was the case with payment of tithe. Thus, by saying that Christ who is a firstfruit is now a tithe, Bishop Cardoso misinterpreted tithe to mean the firstfruit.

Again, it is very erroneous to claim that the Sabbath day is a tithe, and the forbidden tree is a tithe.[9] Mathematically, one day

9. UCKG, *Tithe The Firstfruits.*

out of seven days cannot be a tithe because a tithe is a tenth of a number. If seven days are divided into ten, the result will not be one day. It will be less than one day. Similarly, the forbidden tree being one cannot be a tithe of all the trees in the garden of Eden. One tree can be a tithe of all the trees in the garden if and only if there were only ten trees in the garden. Either UCKG Helpcenter were privy to the number of trees in the garden, or they did not get their tithing mathematics right.

MISCONCEPTION

Do we give or pay tithe?

> It is not accurate to say, "I give tithe"- rather, we should say, "I bring the tithe", since we cannot give what does not belong to us.[10] God may at times allow you to be in a situation where you will have to choose between paying the tithe and leaving the other commitments or keeping the other commitments and not paying the tithe.[11]

Scriptural Position

Bishop Cardoso opines that you "bring" the tithe, not "give" it. I would have agreed with his position if he had argued that that was the case because tithe under the law was not a gift but a mandatory payment, unlike the case before the law. Thus, I disagree with the argument he proffered in support of his position. The word "give" applies to both gifts and payments as well as actions and other categories.[12] Similarly, the word "bring" can apply to both what belongs to you and what does not belong to you. You can bring your property or gift to someone if the recipient did not, or is not expected to, come to you to get the gift. For example, when a

10. Cardoso, *Right Way*, 6.
11. Cardoso, *Right Way*, 11.
12. McIntosh, Cambridge Advanced Learner's.

subject brings a present or gift to a ruler or king. You can also bring a gift, donation, or present to the house of the intended beneficiaries like orphans, fiancé, friends, and relatives.

The word "bring" also applies to objects that do not belong to you but to the recipient. You can bring somebody's property to him or her. Sometime you may not be bound by any law to bring someone else's belonging to him or her. The owner also may not have the power to force you to return his or her property. For example, when you find any lost property and bring it to the owner. In other cases, there may be a statute demanding that you return somebody's property to him or her and that person may be vested with the authority and power to enforce compliance. For example, when you pay your tax to the government, you bring your tax to the government and the government has the power to punish you if you fail to do so. When you bring the tax, you are fulfilling a law; you pay it. Payment has to do with a legal obligation. You pay a debt, and debt is a legal category. If you fail to pay your debt, it is an offense: robbery. A gift is not a statutory obligation; it is what you do out of a free will.

When you bring the tithe, you do so because you are obligated to do so. It is a payment. It is a debt legally binding on those to whom it related to pay. If they did not pay, it amounted to robbery. Tithe was mandatory or compulsory. That is why those who pay tithes feel guilty when they fail to fulfil their tithing obligations because they think that they are breaking a law. You do not feel guilty when you purpose to give a gift to someone but are not able to do so. You just forget it and hope that you will get another opportunity to do so in the future. This is because a gift is not a legal duty but a free-will choice. Tithe was not a gift; it was a legal payment. So those who brought tithes did not give gifts, they made payments. These payments remunerated and sustained the Levites and priests. Furthermore, Bishop Cardoso contradicted himself when he stated that "The Bible doesn't say you will not be saved if you don't give tithe. God did say, however, that those who don't give tithes are robbing Him."[13]

13. Cardoso, *Right Way*, 7.

On page six, he stated that it is not correct to say that one "gives" tithe. But on page seven, he used the word "give" in reference to tithe instead of "bring." On page six, he said, "bring" rather than "give" tithe because it does not belong to you. On page seven, he used the term "give." Either Bishop Cardoso is confused about the nature and status of tithe or he is deliberately wresting the scriptures. As I pointed out earlier, you do not give tithe, you pay tithe. It is a legal debt binding on those to whom it related. To them, it was robbery if they did not pay. However, whether you bring it or pay it, you should do it exactly in the same manner as Abraham did. No other way is acceptable.

MISCONCEPTION

If I don't pay tithe, I will not be saved.[14]

> The Bible doesn't say you will not be saved if you don't give tithe. God did say, however, that those who don't give tithes are robbing Him . . . The Holy Spirit said through the apostle Paul that thieves shall not inherit the kingdom of God (see 1 Cor., 6:10). Therefore we conclude: If those who rob men will not inherit the kingdom of God, what about those who rob God?[15]

Scriptural Position

Bishop Cardoso rightly pointed out that the Bible does not say that one will not be saved if one did not pay tithe. That is true. The Bible did not in any way either directly or indirectly, implicitly or explicitly, say that giving tithe is a requisite condition for salvation. Salvation comes only by faith in the finished work accomplished by Christ on the cross. On the contrary, Bishop Cardoso, as many other contemporary advocates of tithing conflated Malachi 3:8–9

14. Cardoso, *Right Way*, 7.
15. Cardoso, *Right Way*, 7–8.

and First Corinthians 6:10 to conclude that those who did not pay tithe will not inherit the kingdom of God because they robbed God. This amounts to salvation by tithe, which is an insult or blasphemy against God. This is either a deliberate attempt to conjure and instill undue fear in the believers or it is a lack of proper understanding of the scriptures.

As we shall see later, tithes were meant for the Old Testament and had nothing to do with salvation. Robbing God by not paying tithe was in the Old Testament and the curse that followed also pertained to Old Testament believers. Furthermore, the curse was not a curse that damned [the Old Testament] believer but a curse that affected the material prosperity of the [Old Testament] believers. The curse of Malachi 3:8–9 is not the same as the curse of Genesis chapter 2 which damned mankind to eternal destruction. For example, in Genesis 2:16–17, the scriptures say:

> And the LORD God commanded the man, saying, "Of every tree of the garden you may freely eat; but of the tree of the knowledge of good and evil you shall not eat, for in the day that you eat of it you shall surely die.

Again in Ezekiel 18:4, the Lord says: "Behold all souls are Mine; The soul of the father as well as the soul of the son is Mine; The soul who sins shall die." These statements and the curses implied in them are related to the damnation of the soul. It must be pointed out that this curse is all-encompassing because it has both the spiritual as well as the material consequences. Sin brought about both spiritual loss (damnation of soul) and material loss (poverty, sickness, lack.). However, when a sinner turns to God and repents, he or she shall be saved. Ezekiel 18:21–22 says:

> But if a wicked man turns from all his sins which he has committed, keeps all My statutes, and does what is lawful and right, he shall surely live; and not die. None of the transgressions which he has committed shall be remembered against him; because of the righteousness which he has done, he shall live.

A believer may suffer a material loss if he or she is stingy and not generous with the things that God has blessed him or her with. The word of God in Proverbs 11:24–25 says:

> There is one who scatters, yet increases more; and there is one who withholds more than is right, but it leads to poverty. The generous soul will be made rich, and he who waters will also be watered himself.

This is the law of sowing and reaping. Whatever a man sows that shall he reap. If you sow generously, you will reap bountifully. But if you sow sparingly, you will also reap sparingly. Likewise, if you do not sow at all, sorry! There will be nothing to reap. You consumed the seeds you were supposed to sow. Let us return to Malachi 3:8–9 once again.

The curse in Malachi 3:8–9 has nothing to do with the damnation of the soul or salvation. It relates to only the material poverty of the believer or otherwise his or her prosperity. Thus when the Old Testament believers did not pay their tithes, they were exposed to the curse of a devourer who destroyed their livelihoods. That curse was taken away whenever they obeyed the word of God by paying their tithes because God promised in Malachi 3:10–11:

> Bring all the tithes into the storehouse, that there may be food in My house, and try Me now in this . . . if I will not open for you the windows of heaven and pour out for you such blessings that there will not be room enough to receive it. And I will rebuke the devourer for your sakes, so that he will not destroy the fruit of your ground, nor the vine fail to bear fruit for you in the field, says the LORD of hosts.

Even so, in the New Testament, not paying tithe will not hinder anyone from inheriting the kingdom of God because tithing is not a condition for salvation. If non-payment of tithe can damn the soul, then it would be a sin not to pay tithe, because only sin can take one out of the kingdom of God. Galatians 5:19–21 stipulates the things that will damn the soul:

> Now the works of the flesh are evident, which are: adultery, fornication, uncleanness, lewdness, idolatry, sorcery, hatred, contentions, jealousies, outburst of wrath, selfish ambitions, dissensions, heresies, envy, murders, drunkenness, revelries, and the like; of which I tell you beforehand, just as I also told you in time past, that those who practice such things will not inherit the kingdom of God.

This is further emphasized in Revelation 21:8 thus:

> But the cowardly, unbelieving, abominable, murderers, sexually immoral, sorcerers, idolaters, and all liars shall have their part in the lake which burns with fire and brimstone, which is the second death.

If the Bible did not say that one would not be saved for not paying tithe, as Bishop Cardoso affirms, then it is not a sin not to pay tithe. Even though commanded in the Old Testament, tithe was never one of the sacrifices made for the atonement for sin. It only related to God's material blessings and the appropriate distribution of blessings and societal welfare.

The priests and Levites had no inheritance in Israel, so God commanded that they share in, and be maintained with the prosperity of Israel. One way of doing this was by the children of Israel paying tithes to the priests and Levites (Deut 18:1–5). The law of tithing did not specify that defaulters would perish but that they may lose the material blessings of God, as the devourer would attack their livelihoods. Moreover, the sustenance of the priests and Levites did not depend on tithes alone as Deuteronomy 18:3–5 shows:

> And this shall be the priest's due from the people, from those who offer a sacrifice, whether it is bull or sheep: they shall give to the priest the shoulder, the cheek, and the stomach. The firstfruits of your grain and your new wine and your oil, and the first of the fleece of your sheep, you shall give him. For the LORD your God has chosen him out of all your tribes to stand to minister in the name of the LORD, him and his sons forever.

Thus, even though tithes constituted a substantial part of the revenue of the priests and Levites, not paying tithe was not a soul damning offense. Likewise, in the New Testament, not paying tithe does not damn your soul or cancel your salvation "For by grace you have been saved through faith, and that not of yourselves; it is the gift of God, not of works, lest anyone should boast" (Eph 2:8–9).

MISCONCEPTION

Is tithe part of the Law of Moses that was fulfilled and cancelled by Jesus?[16]

> Not at all. The practice of tithing exists since The Creation, long before the Law of Moses. Then it was regulated by the Mosaic Law and further endorsed by the Lord Jesus. Abraham paid tithe, Jacob paid tithe, Abel paid tithe, and they all lived before the Law of Moses.[17]

Scriptural Position

Tithing was an ancient practice that existed at least 430 years before the law. It was incorporated into the law to enforce the welfare of the Levites and priests who were supposed not to have an inheritance in Israel, as well as orphans, widows, and strangers (migrants). God knew that if there were no legal provisions for tithing the people of Israel would not take it seriously, just as Malachi chapter three reported that they did. This was because before the law tithing was not binding on people, it was voluntary. Again, under the law, people did not have regenerated hearts, the new man that is created in true righteousness that willingly serves God without compulsion (Eph 4:24). But God promised to give the New Testament believer a new heart, a heart that seeks and serves

16. Cardoso, *Right Way*, 7.

17. Cardoso, *Right Way*, 7.

God in spirit and truth through faith, and not by enforcement of law. Let us consider some of the names Bishop Cardoso mentioned as paying tithe in the scriptures.

Abraham Gave

Abraham in Genesis "gave" a tithe to Melchizedek. It was a free-will gift that Abraham gave Melchizedek. He was not under any legal obligation to do so, nor was he under any compulsion to do so since there was no law binding him to it. Tithing became a legal and mandatory duty only under the law of Moses. So Abraham did not pay tithe but "gave" it. It was his free-will choice to give a tithe to the priest of God who met him on his return from battle. To further buttress that tithing before the law was voluntary, the Bible records that Jacob vowed to give a tithe of all that God would bless him with.

Jacob Vowed

> Then Jacob made a vow, saying, "If God will be with me, and keep me in this way that I am going, and give me bread to eat and clothing to put on, so that I come back to my father's house in peace, then the LORD shall be my God. And this stone which I have set as a pillar shall be God's house, and of all that You give me I will surely give a tenth to You (Gen 28:20–22).

If tithing was obligatory on believers before the law, then Jacob would not have bound himself with a vow. A vow is a promise, not a duty or payment. However, once a vow is made it becomes obligatory and binding only on the person who made the vow. If tithing was binding before the law, Jacob would not have vowed to give the tenth, rather he would have simply complied or fulfilled the obligation. On the other hand, tithe under the law was a religious duty and a payment.

Abel Offered

It is important also to point out that the offering that Abel brought to the Lord was not a tithe. If it were a tithe it would have been the tenth part of the increase of all his flock and not just the firstborn of his flock (Gen 4:4). Bishop Cardoso will have to agree with me on this except he is suggesting that the tithe was not a tenth part of the tither's revenue.

At the same time Abel brought his offering, his brother Cain also brought an offering to God of the fruits of the ground. He brought an offering just as his brother did but his offering was not accepted by God. If their offerings were tithes, Cain's offering would certainly have been accepted because it would have been the correct portion or tenth part of his harvest. But because what they brought was not tithe, God had to accept or otherwise reject their offerings depending on the state of their hearts and whether their offerings met the demand of faith on the Lamb slain before the foundation of the earth. These two conditions were met by Abel. First, he gave God the first place in his life which he showed by sacrificing the firstborn, the very first of his flock. God saw that. Second, faith was evident in Abel's offering which was a lamb whose life-blood was poured out for Abel.

Cain Also Offered

Cain's offering was great but it did not satisfy the two criteria of faith. His offering was not a firstfruit, and it had no life, no blood to atone for him. While Abel came to God with the blood of the lamb, Cain came with the works of his hand. God also saw that. The offerings of the two brothers had nothing to do with tithe.

We can see that tithing has not always been from creation. Although it existed before the law, it came with the office of the priest and was first mentioned in connection to Abraham and Melchizedek who was a priest.

Christ Endorsed?

Christ did not endorse tithing as Bishop Cardoso claims. He also did not teach it. He brought the issue of tithing into proper perspective when he engaged the Pharisees:

> But woe to you Pharisees! For you tithe mint and rue and all manner of herbs, and pass by justice and the love of God. These you ought to have done without leaving the other undone (Luke 11:42).

When Christ told the Pharisees not to neglect to pay tithe, he did so in the context that the New Testament had not yet come into force and the office of the priests and that of the Levites were still intact and in effect. As long as the Old Testament priests and the Levites were functional, tithe was still necessary. But as soon as Christ shed his blood and the New Testament was established the office of the priest and Levites became redundant or abolished.

Christ never taught tithing, at least from recorded scriptures, and if we, as believers must stay within the written word of God, then we must acknowledge that Christ never taught his followers to pay tithes. He told the Pharisees not to neglect to pay tithe, and the Pharisees were not Christians. He rebuked the Pharisees for tithing everything including the minutest herbs and spices. According to the law, they should tithe everything even the herbs and spices but Christ made it clear that tithing is not important for salvation. What is important is the love of God as well as justice. In this Christ set aside or cancelled tithing. Peter also reiterated the futility of laws and traditions on the one hand, and the redemptive power of the blood of Jesus the Lamb on the other hand "knowing that you were not redeemed with corruptible things, like silver or gold, from your aimless conduct received by tradition from your fathers, but with the precious blood of Christ, as a lamb without blemish and without spot" (1 Pet 1:18–19).

Although the Bible did not record that Christ paid tithe at any time, it will not be wrong to assume that he did because he came to fulfill the law for us. He said that not a tittle or jot of the law shall not be fulfilled (Matt 5:17–18). Fulfilled by who?

Fulfilled by Christ of course. Yet, he berated the Pharisees for tith-ing practically every piece of item. His berating of the Pharisees indicates that tithe is of little importance to Christ. He berated the Pharisees for attaching too great significance to tithe, which was commanded but paid little attention to righteousness, forgiveness, mercy, and justice, which the law could not impart. The virtues that the Pharisees neglected are the virtues that one acquires from Christ through faith. No law can decree or enforce forgiveness or mercy. They are freely given by a worthy benefactor (for example, God) and received by an undeserving beneficiary (for example, humans).

For the Pharisees, one had to tithe even the smallest herb. Today Christians are taught how to tithe every smallest income even if it is a child's support grant.[18] For these New Testament "Pharisees," their received tradition of tithing even an anise is more important, but to Christ it is of no significance. The same goes for other traditions and ancient practices.

Christ, Traditions and Ancient Practices

There were many other traditions and ancient practices that Christ took part in but which he neither endorsed nor were they practiced by the early Christians. For example, circumcision was practiced before the law, incorporated into the law and as a Jew, Christ must have been circumcised on the eighth day. Did Christ teach circum-cision? Did the early Church enforce circumcision? We know the answer is "no." Again the feast of harvest (firstfruits) was instituted under the law. But before the law, Abel brought the firstborn of his flock as a sacrifice to God. Also, God demanded that Abraham sacrifice his son Isaac who was the first male to open Sarah's womb. He was a firstfruit. The feast of the firstfruits continued as a Jewish tradition and Christ no doubt would have taken part in it. Yet, he neither taught it nor was it carried over to the New Testament.

18. Cardoso, Right Way.

Similarly, Sabbath worship did not start with the law. The Bible clearly stated that God did the work of creation in six days and he rested on the seventh day and hallowed it. The Sabbath day worship was enunciated under the law. Did Christ worship on the Sabbath day? Of course, he did. Did he teach that Christians worship on the Sabbath day? No! Did early Christians make it binding to worship on the Sabbath day? No! The Holy Spirit through Paul taught that there is no special day before God. Whatever day anyone chooses to worship God is acceptable to God. The worship of God is a daily, continuous, personal, and spiritual state of affairs. The gathering of the saints together at a place is for God to nourish us with his word through his servants, and for us to fellowship with and encourage one another. This is where the day of worship becomes relevant. As Romans 14:5–6 states "One person esteems one day above another; another esteems every day alike. Let each be fully convinced in his own mind. He who observes the day, observes it to the Lord; and he who does not observe the day, to the Lord he does not observe it."

These traditions of tithing, firstfruit, and Sabbath started before the law, were incorporated into the law, fulfilled by Christ but were not accepted as part of the Christian New Testament because Christ set them aside.

Why Did Christ Observe Traditions If He Did Not Endorse Them?

Why would Christ practice traditions and fulfill laws that he would not prescribe for the New Testament believers? The answer is that he had to take part in them to fulfill the law (for us), which he came to do. Likewise, he did not endorse nor teach tithing. Tithing was not the only ancient practice that was recorded in the Bible. Most preachers of today hold unto tithing for material benefit. They are exploiting or making merchandise of believers (2 Pet 2:3).

The early Christians never practiced tithing as claimed by today's preachers. All references made by preachers to tithe in the church today are based on the Old Testament or lifted out of context from the New Testament. All the New Testament scriptures cited by preachers in support of their doctrines on tithing refer to the maintenance of the ministers of the gospel; and all the Bible verses in the New Testament relating to material supplies for ministers refer to offerings and gifts which are voluntary. All the arguments to support tithing are based on indirect Bible references, conflations, and incorrect inferences.

MISCONCEPTION

Tithes And Offerings: The Blood Of The Church.[19]

> It is the Holy Spirit who guides His Church. He reveals the Kingdom of God to the world. However, the Church of the Lord Jesus Christ would never be able to spread the Gospel of Salvation to the nations if it weren't for an indispensable tool: money. It was precisely for this reason that God established the law of tithes and offerings in the Church.
> We understand that money is for the Church what blood is for the human body. Money makes it possible to receive eternal life wherever they are: at home, in hospital, in prison, etc. Billions of people will spend eternity in hell simply because no one told them about salvation through Jesus Christ. And if there was no one to tell them about Jesus, it's because there was no one to finance the missionary work through their tithes and offerings.[20]

Scriptural Position

The first error that needs to be pointed out from the above quote is the conflation of tithe with money. As stated in chapter one, money was never used for tithing. Only agricultural produce were used. The leap or conversion from tithing agricultural produce to

19. UCKG, *Tithe the Firstfruits*, 18.
20. UCKG, *Tithe the Firstfruits*, 18.

tithing money is one that has no basis in the scriptures. Having stated that, let us address the misconception in question.

Money is the Blood of the Church

The claim that money is the blood of the church draws upon the same source as other erroneous teachings as "tithers are financial pillars of God's house" (see page 38). This claim is very pernicious if not blasphemous because it attributes the work of the Holy Spirit to man and mammon. It is a ridiculous travesty to claim that the church of the Lord Jesus Christ would "never" be able to spread the gospel to the nations without money which is exalted to the height of an "indispensable tool." At no time has the church of Jesus Christ depended on money for the evangelization of the world. Even today, the preaching of the gospel has depended less on money than on the obedience of the disciples of Christ to share the good news as commanded by the Master. It is only the Holy Spirit that is indispensable in the spread of the gospel, not money. When Christians obey the Master, the Holy Spirit works with them. To teach them that their missions and ministries did not, and should not depend on money, Jesus told his disciples to carry no money bag (Luke 10:4). Jesus knew that in the last days, false teachers whose god is their belly (Phil 3:19) will arise and by covetousness exploit and make merchandize of believers (2 Pet 2:3). To such false teachers, and the church of mammon, money is certainly indispensable but not to the church of Jesus Christ.

God Established the Law of tithes and Offering in the Church

It has been claimed that precisely because tithes and offerings are the blood of the church, God established the law of tithes and offerings in the church. This is not the case. First, God did not establish any law of tithing and offering in the church. Second, the law of tithing and offering was not established for the evangelization of the nations. Tithing was commanded in respect of the Old

Testament Levitical priesthood and not for the New Testament church. As for offerings both in the Old and New Testaments, there is no law or commandment as to how a believer should give (see Not by Commandment, page 63). Offerings are freewill gifts in both Testaments.

Money Makes Eternal Life Possible

It has also been claimed that money makes it possible for people to receive eternal life wherever they are, whether at home, in hospital, in prison, or any other place. This, again, is not true. Salvation is by grace "through faith, and that not of yourselves; it is the gift of God, not of works, lest anyone should boast" (Eph 2:8–9). God can and has saved souls everywhere without money being spent. Cornelius was saved at home (Acts 10), Saul of Tarsus was saved on his way to Damascus (Acts 9), an Ethiopian eunuch was saved on his journey from Jerusalem back home (Acts 8:26–40), Lydia was saved by a riverside (Acts 16:13–15), and a jailer was saved in his own prison (Acts 16:23–32). Many more were saved on their sickbed, at home, in the synagogues, in the cities, in the country-side, by the seashore, and divers places as Jesus and his disciples ministered, healed the sick, and fed the multitudes. All these great deeds and missions were accomplished without any tithes and offerings. Therefore, it is not true that "Billions of people will spend eternity in hell simply because no one told them about salvation through Jesus Christ . . . because there was no one to finance the missionary work through their tithes and offerings."

Chapter 3

THE CAUSE FOR THE COLLECTION

FOR WHAT CAUSE IS tithe paid and collected? Is tithe for ministers or for the ministry? There are two broad groups of tithing ministers. The first group of tithing ministers are those who use tithes for work of their ministries, be it schools, clinics, church buildings, charity, or evangelization. They do not use tithes or offerings as their private income. They also give their own tithes just like any other tither. They honestly believe that tithe is for the work of God and therefore use it for the same. Whether they are right or wrong in their interpretation of the scriptures on tithing is not the question here. What is important here is that they do not use the people of God or the gospel as a means of enriching themselves.

The second group comprises preachers who believe that tithes are for the exclusive consumption of the ministers and those they permit the rare privilege of enjoying it with them. They may give tithe or not, but at the end of the day, the tithe belongs to them. It is their remuneration for the work of the gospel to be used for their luxury and private empires. This chapter looks at what the ministers do with the tithes they receive.

SUPPORT PRESENT-DAY LEVITES

According to the advocates of tithing, tithes are used for several purposes in the church. One of such purposes in their view is to support the worship team because they are the present-day Levites. They used Second Chronicles 5:12 to support this claim. For them, tithe is used to support and maintain musicians in the church. Let us not flog the fact that musicians in the churches today can, and do have a music careers apart from the church worship ministry. However, the questions that beg for answers are: were Levites musicians? Is singing the primary God-assigned responsibility of the Levites? Numbers 3:5–38 identifies the three clans of the Levites—Gershon, Kohath, and Merari—and stipulates their duties. There was no mention of any of them being assigned the duty of singing.

The mention of Levites as singers was in respect of the appointment made by King David and that was from a particular set of families from the clan of Merari and the clan of the Kohath, and none from the clan of Gershon (I Chr 6:29–33, 15:16–17). These singers were to sing on specific special occasions, but singing was not the primary calling of the Levites. However, assuming that singing was one of their duties in the Old Testament, then they were legitimately remunerated with their appointed share of tithes because they did not have any other source of income. But in the New Testament, where church musicians pursue private careers, and in some cases, so many careers at the same time, are they entitled to tithe?

Again, if we collect tithes to support a segment of Levites, that is, musicians in the church, what should we do about the other sets of Levites—those who carry the ark of the covenant, those who set up the tabernacle for the ark and dismantle it when the ark is carried out? These we can liken to ushers and church workers who labor to set up the stage for the minister to preach. Are these not Levites? I have not heard any preacher tell us that these children of God who volunteer their time and energy to the service of God receive financial support in terms of tithe. If they don't, why are musicians in the church now the Levites who are entitled to tithes but these other workers are not Levites, and why are they not equally entitled to the same benefit? Or are the proponents of paying church musicians saying that only one family from Merari clan and one family from Kohath clan who happened to be blessed with the gift of singing constituted the entirety of Levites? Or are they "more Levites than others?"

Equally interesting is the position of Bishop Cardoso on the purposes of tithe. According to him:

> God established tithes not only for the purpose of bless-ing His people but also to provide for the needs of His House. "That there may be food in My House" (Malachi 3:10). Tithers are the financial pillars of God's House. It's because of their faithfulness that Church can pay its existing expenses and plan to expand the work of God. Your tithes are directly used for these purposes.[1]

FOOD IN GOD'S HOUSE

I agree with Bishop Cardoso that God instituted the tithe to pro-vide for the needs of his house. However, I will also point out that these needs are limited to the material needs of the ministers of the altar and the sanctuary (the priests and Levites) not the needs of the ministry. "That there may be food in My House" means "that there may be food for the priests and Levites to eat." The relevant tithes pertained only to the welfare of the priests and Levites: what to eat and what to wear. Likewise, the third type of tithe is for the consumption of the tithers themselves. The fourth kind of tithe pertains to the welfare of the orphans, widows, and strangers (mi-grants) who constituted the poor. All these categories of people make up the House of God: the priests and Levites, the people of God, and the widows, orphans and strangers. These groups were imperfect symbolic representations of the various groups of believ-ers in the New Testament, that is, the ministers, the members of the church which include the third group, the poor in the church.

1. Cardoso, *Right Way*, 13.

In the New Testament, every believer is called to be a minister. The work of the ministry is not reserved for a special set of people. We all are members of the house of God. We are of the family of God. Shouldn't we all partake of tithe? The early church left us an example of how to live as a family. Nobody paid tithes, rather, they had all things in common (Acts 2:44–46).

FINANCIAL PILLARS

The view that tithers are financial pillars of God's house is an off-shoot or extension of an earlier claim and misconception that tithes and offerings converted to money are the blood of the church. Both in the Old Testament and New Testament, tithers have never been financial pillars in the house of God. Perhaps, they may be pillars for today's preachers, not for God. In the Old Testament, they paid tithes as of law and everybody did pay tithe. So nobody occupied a special position of a financial pillar in the house of God. In the New Testament, there was no evidence that believers paid tithes, nor were commanded to do so except in the interpretation, conflations, and inferences of contemporary preachers.

The church has never depended and should not depend on tithes to pay for its expenses, and the execution or expansion of the work of God. Whether in the Old Testament or the New Testament, the work of God has never depended on tithes or offerings collected on days of worship. God has always provided for his work. A few examples will suffice here.

Abraham's Sacrifice

In Genesis 22:8, 13–14, it is written how God provided Abraham with a lamb for sacrifice:

> And Abraham said, "My son, God will provide for Him-self the lamb for a burnt offering." So the two of them went together. Then Abraham lifted his eyes and looked, and there behind him was a ram caught in a thicket by its

horns. So Abraham went and took the ram, and offered it up for a burnt offering instead of his son. And Abraham called the name of the place, The-LORD-Will-Provide; as it is said to this day, "In the Mount of the LORD it shall be provided.

Building the Tabernacle and Setting up the Priesthood

The greatest work of the house of God in the wilderness was the building of the tabernacle and the institution of the priesthood. God did not ask the children of Israel to bring a tithe. Remember, tithe was not a new concept at this time. The concept of tithe has been common knowledge for at least 430 years before this time. Rather God asked them to bring a freewill offering:

> Then the LORD spoke to Moses, saying: Speak to the children of Israel, that they bring Me an offering. From everyone who gives it willingly with his heart you shall take My offering. And this is the offering which you shall take from them: gold, silver and bronze; blue, purple, and scarlet thread, fine linen, and goats' hair; ram skins dyed red, badger skins, and acacia wood; oil for the light, and spices for the anointing oil and for the sweet incense; onyx stones, and stones to be set in the ephod and in the breastplate. And let them make Me a sanctuary, that I may dwell among them (Exod 25:1–8).

The offering or service that God desires is that which is given willingly from the heart "in spirit and in truth." There was no other project more important in the life of the children of Israel at this stage than the building of the tabernacle, yet God did not levy a tithe on them to raise funds. God dictated in detail all the materials required, from gold to wood; from bars to pins, which were all provided by willing, generous, grateful, and cheerful worshipers. They even brought more than required:

> Then everyone came whose heart was stirred, and everyone whose spirit was willing, and they brought the LORD's offering for the work of the tabernacle of

meeting, for all its service, and for the holy garments. The children of Israel brought a freewill offering to the LORD, all men and women whose heart were willing to bring material for all kinds of work which the LORD, by the hand of Moses, had commanded to be done (Exod 35:21, 29).

Then all the craftsmen who were doing all the work of the sanctuary came, each from the work he was doing, and spoke to Moses, saying, "The people bring much more than enough for the service of the work which the LORD commanded us to do." So Moses gave a commandment, and they caused it to be proclaimed throughout the camp, saying, "Let neither man nor woman do any more work for the offering of the sanctuary." And the people were restrained from bringing, for the material they had was sufficient for all the work to be done—indeed too much (Exod 36:4–7).

Solomon's Temple

Another time when the work of the house of the Lord was done was when Solomon built the Temple. Second Chronicles 3:1–2 states: "Now Solomon began to build the house of the LORD at Jerusalem on Mount Moriah, where the LORD appeared to his father David, at the place that David had prepared on the threshing floor of Ornan the Jebusite."

This was not with the tithe of the people of Israel but with what has already been provided by David the father of Solomon. After this Temple was vandalized, King Joash repaired it, not with tithes but with the voluntary contributions of the generous, joyful, and cheerful people of God. Second Chronicles 24:4, 9, 12, 14 records that:

> Now it happened after this that Joash set his heart on repairing the house of the LORD. And they made a proclamation throughout Judah and Jerusalem to bring to the LORD the collection that Moses the servant of God had imposed on Israel in the wilderness. Then the king

and Jehoiadah gave it to those who did the work of the service of the house of the LORD; and they hired masons and carpenters to repair the house of the LORD, and also those who worked in iron and bronze to restore the house of the LORD. When they had finished, they brought the rest of the money before the king and Jehoadah; they made from it articles for the house of the LORD, articles for serving and offering, spoons and vessels of gold and silver. And they offered burnt offerings in the house of the LORD continually all the days of Jehoiadah.

The examples above happened in the Old Testament, one before the law and the other under the law. None of the projects was executed with tithes. One thing that is outstanding from these incidents is that whenever believers give willingly for the work of God, there is always abundance, more than the work required, hence a leftover of materials.

In the New Testament, the early church did not charge tithes. The Bible says that they had all things in common and everyone who had a property sold it and brought the proceeds to the church, and this was distributed as believers had needs (Acts 4:32–35). Again, when there was a famine that affected the whole world, the church, particularly of the gentiles, supported the church in Judea as "the disciples, each according to his ability, determined to send relief to the brethren dwelling in Judea" (Acts 11:29). They did not send tithes. It was always a freewill offering as they chose, that is, as they determined to give.

Similarly, the ministry of evangelizing the world by the early church was not accomplished with the tithes of believers. Apostle Paul who evangelized more than any other apostle did not charge any fees for the work of the gospel. In fact, he was reluctant to accept the freewill gifts of the churches that he founded. Paul was aware of his rights to the entitlements of the ministers of the gospel as he told the Corinthians "that those who minister the holy things eat of the things of the temple, and those who serve at the altar partake of the offerings of the altar? Even so the Lord has commanded that those who preach the gospel should live from the gospel" (1 Cor 9:13–14).

Two distinct categories are evident from the above scripture. The first category are "those who minister the holy things . . . the things of the temple, and those who serve at the altar." The second category is that of "those who preach the gospel." Members of the first group "partake of the offerings of the altar." The second group "should live from the gospel."

Paul fell into the second category. He was entitled to the material benefits of preaching the gospel. However, Paul did not make himself a burden to anyone or any church. He asked the Corinthian church:

> Do we have no right to eat and drink? Or is it only Barnabas and I who have no right to refrain from working? If we have sown spiritual thing for you, is it a great thing if we reap your material things? If others are partakers of this right over you, are we not even more? Nevertheless we have not used this right, but endure all things lest we hinder the gospel of Christ (1 Cor 9:4, 6, 11–12).

If Paul did not demand the freewill offerings and gifts to which he was entitled, then how would he have accepted tithes. He did not use this right yet he traversed the then known world preaching the gospel of Jesus Christ. I have been in the church long enough to know that churches have not depended on tithes for survival, and the work of God has not depended on the same to be accomplished. I have never heard any preacher claim that the church could not survive without tithes, or that the work of God could not be done without tithes, or that souls could not be won to the Lord because there was no tithe to finance evangelization. Even the construction of church buildings has not depended on tithes.

GOD'S WORK DOES NOT DEPEND ON TITHES

Concrete evidence must be presented to show that the so-called "work of God" does not necessarily depend on tithes. Whenever there was any project in any church that required finances, the believers have always been asked to make offerings: donations or contributions towards the specific projects. The very same scriptures cited above (Exod 25:1–8, 35:21–29, 36:4–7) are often used to encourage believers to give for the work of God. However, these scriptures do not refer to tithes. Again, if believers are asked to make special contributions for major projects in the house of God, then why do preachers still ask for tithes? For the same so-called "work of God." The church can, and has always survived without tithes. But it does seem that contemporary preachers cannot survive without tithes. That is why they have elevated it to a status at par with grace. For them, a person gets saved by believing in Christ on one hand and by paying tithes on the hand. For them, if one did not pay tithes, one will end up in hell.

Chapter 4

THE COVENANTS AND
THEIR COMMANDMENTS

THE OLD AND NEW covenants are markedly different in respect of tithe. In the Old Testament, tithe was central to the sustenance of the Levitical priesthood and social welfare in the nation of Israel. In the New Testament, tithe was not taught nor endorsed by Christ. It was also not practiced by the apostles. The recorded traditions of the early church testify to this. The early church did not segregate between the apostle and the "ordinary" church members when it came to sharing things in the house of God. They had all things in common. They saw themselves as one body, which had no consideration or respect for people's status, whether rich or poor, Jews or Gentiles, preachers or parishioners. For example, when the Holy Spirit descended on them on the day of Pentecost, he did not first come upon the apostle before the rest of the believers, neither did he give the apostles a double portion of the tongue of fire. But he blessed all of them equally. That is God in the New Testament.

In the Old Testament, it was not like that. The Spirit of God came upon only those who were called by God for special assignments like kings, prophets, and priests. For example, when Saul was anointed the king of Israel, the Spirit of God came upon him causing him to prophesy (1 Sam 10:1–13). Again, in the Old

Testament, not everyone entered the innermost sanctuary, the holy of holies, the priest did, and that only once a year. Not everyone ruled as king, only the anointed kings did. But in the New Testament, all believers are both kings and priests, hence, "royal priesthood."

DIFFERENCES BETWEEN OLD TESTAMENT PRIESTS AND NEW TESTAMENT PRIESTS

There are some differences between the Old Testament (Levitical) priests and the New Testament priest:

Many Old versus One New

The Old Testament priests were many. Hebrews 7:23 says, "Also there were many priests, because they were prevented by death from continuing." They were mortals subject to death and were replaced when they died. The New Testament priest is one and immortal. He lives forever and is sitting at the right hand of the father. "But He, because He continues forever, has an unchangeable priesthood" (Heb 7:24). "Now this is the main point of the things we are saying: We have such a High Priest, who is seated at the right hand of the throne of the Majesty in the heavens" (Heb 8:1). This priest is one and all of us that are saved are his members, that is, "parts of his body."

Imperfect and Temporary Old versus Perfect and Permanent New

The Old Testament priesthood due to its imperfection was a temporary institution:

> Therefore, if perfection were through the Levitical priesthood (for under it the people received the law), what further need was there that another priest should rise according to the order of Melchizedek, and not be called

according to the order of Aaron? for the law made nothing perfect; on the other hand, there is the bringing in of a better hope, through which we draw near to God (Heb 7:11, 19).

The Old Testament priesthood was set aside when Christ died on the cross and the veil in the temple tore from top to down revealing and opening the gate of life to as many as will receive Christ to access the presence of God. The job of the Old Testament priest ended at this point. We no longer need any intermediary to mediate between man and God. We can now come to God with boldness, as we all are now made priests by Christ and in Christ.

Unlike the Old Testament priesthood, the New Testament priesthood is permanent and eternal. It is the perfect priesthood, which replaced the imperfect Old Testament priesthood. The High Priest of the New Testament, the Lord Jesus Christ, is an eternal priest, and his priesthood is in the order of Melchizedek, without beginning or end.

Natural Old versus Spiritual New

The Old Testament priesthood was a human priesthood constituted of natural men, who ministered on altars made by natural hands, of natural materials—such as wood, gold, silver, and bronze—upon which were offered sacrifices of natural farm produce and animals. The New Testament priesthood is founded on the divinity of Christ "who has come, not according to the law of a fleshly commandment, but according to the power of an endless life" (Heb 7:16). Furthermore, Hebrews 9:11–12 says:

> But Christ came as High Priest of the good things to come, with greater and more perfect tabernacle not made with hands, that is, not of this creation. Not with the blood of goats and calves, but with His own blood He entered the Most Holy Place once and for all, having obtained eternal redemption.

Christ offered his life-blood once and for all, and through him, we that are redeemed offer sacrifices of praise and cheerful and holy worship on the altar that is not made with hands or natural things. It is a spiritual priesthood and all the redeemed are members of the priesthood. Hence, "You also, as living stones, are being built up a spiritual house, a holy priesthood, to offer up spiritual sacrifices acceptable to God through Jesus Christ" (1 Pet 2:5).

Earthly Old versus Heavenly New

The Old Testament priesthood was instituted to minister on earth because "the first covenant had ordinances of divine service and earthly sanctuary" (Heb 9:1). The priests were the intermediaries and mediators between God the redeemer and the lost man on earth. On the other hand, the New Testament Priest is a heavenly priest: "For if He were on earth, He would not be a priest, since there are priests who offer the gifts according to the law" (Heb 8:4). He is God who came down to redeem and unite humankind with himself so that we can sit with him in heavenly places. The New Testament priesthood does not have room for intermediaries as every believer can equally access God through Jesus Christ "For Christ has not entered the holy places made with hands, which are copies of the true, but into heaven itself, now to appear in the presence of God for us" (Heb 9:24) and "after He had offered one sacrifice for sins forever, sat down at the right hand of God" (Heb 10:12).

Limited Old versus Boundless New

The Old Testament priest was physically bound or limited. Stationed in Israel and physically bottled up in a naturally mortal body, he was in all things limited. Our New Testament priest is not limited. He is omnipotent, omnipresent, and omniscient. He is boundless.

Fallible Old versus Infallible New

The Old Testament priest was fallible. He could make mistakes. He was subject to the law of sin just as those for whom he intermediated. Therefore, he had to make atonement first for his own sins before he could approach God on behalf of others. The New Testament priest is infallible in all things. He never sinned and does not make atonement for himself. His holy blood is all that the Father requires for the redemption of the world.

Dependent Old versus Self-Sufficient New

The Old Testament priesthood was a dependent institution. The priests in the Old Testament were not allowed to work to earn incomes, nor to have possessions like the other children of Israel. They were provided for by the offerings and tithes of the people of Israel. Hence, the tithes were important. The New Testament priesthood is not a dependent priesthood. It is a self-sufficient priesthood. The ministers of this priesthood are allowed to work, earn wages, and own properties in the midst of their brethren. They are not forbidden from anything that the other people can do. Hence, they do not need any tithes to sustain themselves.

WHY CONTEMPORARY PREACHERS CONFLATE THE COVENANTS AND COMMANDMENTS

Now, why do today's preachers emphasize tithing when there are no scriptural foundations for it? Christ gave the answer in Matthew 23:25, 28: "Woe to you scribes and Pharisees, hypocrites! For you cleanse the outside of the cup and dish, but inside they are full of extortion and self-indulgence." Today's preachers present an outward appearance of righteousness and service to God by emphasizing the payment of tithe. But what they are actually doing is extortion of money from church members, and that for one purpose: self-indulgence.

We hear and read about preachers who have properties here and there in the most exclusive and most expensive parts of some cities of the world. Some even have private jets to fly around the world ostensibly "doing the work of God, and ministering the blessing of Abraham to the world." They tell anyone who wants to listen that their "god is not a poor god." But within their churches are many poor people who need help. Instead of distributing the wealth in the church to be a blessing to all its members, they rather indulge themselves in all forms of worldly and self-glorifying ventures, and pleasures. They compete with the world in self-gratification, and they make the church members pay for their carnal indulgences by extorting money from them in the name of tithe.

If you ask any preacher what their church does with tithe, you are sure to hear a number of "work of God" which God has instructed him to accomplish, and which the church must finance. They build private business empires which do not belong to the church but to the preachers. Where these empires belonged to the church, then the church is run as private businesses of the preacher. They lie when they claim that tithe is for the work of God when they are actually building private empires with it. They add to the word of God by teaching what Christ did not command. By appropriating to themselves ungodly proceeds from the gospel and by spending such proceeds on their greed and desires, they turn the pulpit into an altar of mammon.

Christ taught that one cannot serve two masters at the same time. One can serve only God or only mammon at any given time but not the two. Either one serves God in spirit and in truth of the word of God, or one serves mammon in the flesh, and deception and lies. You may serve mammon by any means you may invent, and by any standard you may set up for yourself but it will not be by the standard of the word of God. Christ has taught us how to serve God and by what means we are to execute and support his work.

Chapter 5

THE CHIEF CORNERSTONE

JESUS CHRIST IS THE author and finisher of—that is, the one that perfects—the Christian's faith. He is the foundation on which the Christian builds his beliefs and practices. What Christ taught and practiced on any matter defines, decides, and determines what a Christian should believe and practice on that subject. A Christian must neither add nor deduct from the teaching of Christ on any subject. The word of God declares:

> Now, therefore, you are no longer strangers and foreigners, but fellow citizens with the saints and members of the household of God, having been built on the foundation of the apostles and prophets, Jesus Christ Himself being the chief cornerstone (Eph 2:19–20).

If Christ is the chief cornerstone upon which the Christian faith is built, then the church's teachings and practices on tithing must mirror what Christ taught on it and his practice of it. The question that should decide whether a Christian should pay tithe or not is: "Did Christ, as the eternal priest, demand, collect, or receive tithes?" If the answer to this question is yes, then, the church may demand, collect, and receive tithes. On the other hand, if the answer is no, then, the church has no absolute mandate to demand, collect, or receive tithes.

Proponents of tithing in the New Testament premise their argument on some scriptures which they interpret to mean that Jesus approved of tithing for Christians. One of such scriptures is Matthew 23:23 in which Jesus reprimanded the scribes and Pharisees:

> Woe to you, scribes and Pharisees, hypocrites! For you pay tithe of mint and anise and cumin, and have neglected the weightier matters of the law: justice and mercy and faith. These you ought to have done, without leaving the others undone.

This scripture records a rebuke to the scribes and Pharisees who were the visible representation of Old Testament institutions: the "Law and the prophets." Jesus reproved them for something they did, that is, "pay tithe of mint and anise and cumin." He also chided them for something which they neglected to do, that is, "the weightier matters of the law." He then advised them to both pay tithe, as well as to observe justice, mercy, and faith.

It is this piece of advice that has been (mis)interpreted to mean that Jesus taught that Christians should pay tithe. Their argument is that since Jesus insisted that the scribes and Pharisees ought to pay tithe, then, it means that he approved of tithing in the New Testament. On the contrary, the context within which Jesus made these statements strongly indicates that it was a rebuttal of how the scribes and Pharisees practiced tithing, rather than an approval and endorsement of tithing in the New Testament.

Jesus was addressing the Old Testament believers represented in the scribes and Pharisees. Thus, his advice to pay tithe was directed at the Old Testament believers and not the New Testament church. His advice was in the context that they were still in the Old Testament and the New Testament was yet to come into effect. Thus, the institution of the Levitical priesthood was still in operation and required tithes to sustain as commanded by God. Christ, having come to fulfill the law and the prophets, had to uphold this aspect of the law until it is fulfilled and brought to an end with the establishment of the New Testament. Paul presents Christ as the end of the Old Testament "For they being ignorant of God's righteousness, and seeking to establish their own righteousness, have not submitted to righteousness of God. For Christ is the end of the law for righteousness to everyone who believes" (Rom 10:3–4).

If Christ is the end of the law, how then did he approve of an aspect of the same law which he has brought to an end? Thus, as earlier stated, the Lord did not endorse tithing in the church and the early Christians did not practice it. So what did Jesus teach?

CHRIST'S TEACHING ON OFFERING

In Matthew 5:23–24, Jesus taught: "Therefore if you bring your gift to the altar, and there remember that your brother has something against you, leave your gift there before the altar, and go your way. First be reconciled to your brother, and then come and offer your gift."

Three words are obvious from the scripture above. Those words are "bring," "gift," and "offer." Thus, Christ taught us that our offerings are gifts that we bring to God. A gift is a free-will benevolent gesture, not a payment. Likewise, an offering is not a tithe that is "paid." If the Lord did not approve of payment of tithes as source of church finance or as remunerations to preachers, how are the ministers of the gospel to be remunerated?

Gospel Ministers' Remuneration

The Lord specified how the ministers of the gospel should be remunerated and how the work of the ministry is to be financed. This formed the standard practice for the early church. In Luke 10:4, 5, 7, 8 the Lord commanded the disciples to:

> Carry neither money bag, knapsack, nor sandals; and greet no one along the road. But whatever house you enter, first say, 'Peace to this house.' And remain in the same house, eating and drinking such things as they give, for the laborer is worthy of his wages. Do not go from house

to house. Whatever city you enter, and they receive you,
eat such things as are set before you.

There is no place here or in any other scripture where the
Lord Jesus directly or indirectly even permitted the believers to
pay tithes as wages to ministers of the gospel. The command to
ministers was to eat and drink "such things as they give," that is
"whatever" is set before the minister. If they set a banquette, eat.
If they set a slice of dry bread, eat. If they set an array of the best
drinks before you, drink. If they set a cup of water, also drink. This
is the wage of the minister.

The Lord specifically instructed, "carry no moneybag". In
other words, do not make financial provision for yourself, God
will provide for you. The ministry is not a money-spinning venture
where millionaires are made. It is a high calling for only those who
know that their wages are those offerings, which are willingly set
before them by the sons of peace, that is, the church of God. The
minister's wage is whatever the believers are able, and willing to offer, not what the minister can extort from them by threatening and
frightening them with "you are cursed with a curse" when God
has not cursed them. It must be cheerfully given and cheerfully
received, for freely you received and freely you must give (Matt
10:8). This did not refer to tithes or any form of compulsory payment. What the church can give to a preacher could be "the mil-
lions of the wealthy" or "the mites of the widow." Whatever it is, as
long as it is a voluntary and cheerful offering of the people of God,
then the minister is worthy of it. The church must return to the
true perspective on how God values our services to him. The story
of the widow's mite throws light on how the Lord weighs the gifts
and services of his people.

The Widow's Mites

The story of the widow's mites is recorded like this:

Now Jesus sat opposite the treasury and saw how people
put money into the treasury. And many who were rich

put in much. Then one poor widow came and threw in two mites, which make a quadrans. So He called His disciples to Himself and said to them, 'Assuredly, I say to you that this poor widow has put in more than all those who had given to the treasury; for they all put in out of their abundance, but she out of her poverty put in all that she had, her whole livelihood (Mark 12:41–44).

A number of lessons can be drawn from the story of the widow and her mites. First lesson to learn from the story is that there are practices that are meant for the scribes and Pharisees, and those that are meant for the disciples and the church. This particular message and teaching was for the disciples, not the multitude in the synagogue, not for the Pharisees, and not for the Old Testament priests. When he addressed the tithe question, he spoke to the people it concerned: the scribes and Pharisees, but when he wanted to enunciate heavenly principles "He called His disciples to Himself and said to them." He separated them from the crowd. Second lesson to learn from the story is that Jesus taught his disciples what is acceptable in the kingdom of God which should be practiced in the church. He taught that the kind of offering that is acceptable to God must be willing, cheerful and sacrificial. If the Lord opens our eyes into the hearts of believers today, we are most likely to see people who are giving out of fear and not for the love of God. Hence, when their fears recede they revert to their normal level of giving. So what we have today is a coerced and forced payment, not the willing, cheerful, and sacrificial offering that the Lord loves.

The widow's giving was done willingly. She was not forced by any laws to give. She could as well have refrained from giving at all and still remained a true worshipper of God. But she chose to give all her livelihood. This is a lesson not only in giving our material things but also in the service of God altogether. We are commanded to love the Lord with all our heart, soul, and mind. We have to love and serve the Lord with all we are and all we have, and we must do that willingly. Many of those who pay tithe today do not pay willingly. That is why the preachers keep hammering on tithe regularly. The people have to be motivated, cajoled, and threatened with a curse of some devourers for them to pay their tithes. Thus, they pay tithes but not cheerfully.

The widow's offering was also given cheerfully. She was not grumbling as she was putting her mites in the treasury. Although those were all that she had, she did not complain. She could have grumbled: "I could solve one problem or two with this money but now I have to give it out otherwise God will curse me and the devourer will be after me." No, she never grumbled. Many of the people who pay tithe today complain and grumble. The widow gave cheerfully, otherwise, the Lord would have pointed out that she was not happy giving all her livelihood.

Similarly, the widow also gave sacrificially. It was a sacrifice on her part to have given all that she had. Although she was a poor widow, she did not consider that she needed help herself but counted it all joy to give everything she had so that the work of God will not suffer. She preferred to starve than for the servants of the Lord who had no inheritance and or any means of livelihood to go hungry. She could have tithed her mites, which is not only a reasonable thing to do but also lawful. But she gave all. She knew what the likely consequences of giving up all her livelihood were, yet she went ahead to give her mites. This sacrifice was not after a long frightening sermon on "robbing God and being cursed with a curse." By recognizing and commending the widow and her mites, Jesus taught his disciples how God regards the little but honest, willing, sacrificial, and cheerful offerings. God also maximizes such little but pleasing offerings for large-scale projects.

LARGE-SCALE PROJECTS BY CHRIST

Did Christ execute large scale projects in his days on earth? How did he finance them? A few things the church of today can learn from the Master himself. God does not change, and likewise, his patterns and ways do not change. Just two examples will suffice to explain how the Lord wants his church to conduct herself on earth.

Feeding of Multitudes

Matthew 14:14–21 records:

> And when Jesus went out He saw a great multitude; and He was moved with compassion for them, and healed their sick. When it was evening, His disciples came to Him, saying, "This is a deserted place, and the hour is already late. Send the multitudes away, that they may go into the villages and buy themselves food." But Jesus said to them, "They do not need to go away. You give them something to eat." And they said to Him, "We have here only five loaves and two fish." He said, "Bring them here to Me." Then He commanded the multitudes to sit down on the grass. And He took the five loaves and the two fish, and looking up to heaven, He blessed and broke and gave the loaves to the disciples; and the disciples gave to the multitudes. So they all ate and were filled, and they took up twelve baskets full of the fragments that remained. Now those who had eaten were about five thousand men, besides women and children.

This story narrates one of the greatest project management event in the Bible. The circumstances surrounding this event were such that it was logistically impossible to successfully execute considering the multitude involved and the limited time frame. Yet again, the Lord used this event to teach the important, and critical ingredients, and requirements for the work of God to be successfully carried out.

Vision

The first requirement for a successful mission is the vision of the field. Jesus saw the multitude; a multitude that needed love, compassion, and help. He did not see potential tithers. He did not see potential sources of wealth, and profligate lifestyle. Jesus saw a multitude of broken, sick, oppressed, and needy people. He saw precious souls to be won for the kingdom of God at all costs, even if it meant spending and being spent. Thus, the way a minister sees the field will determine how he will react or respond to the people, whether with carelessness or compassion. The disciples saw a different field from the one Jesus saw. They saw a multitude of burdens but Jesus saw a multitude of hungry souls.

Compassion

The second ingredient for successful mission is compassion. Jesus was moved with compassion for the multitude. Compassion brings about healings both of the body and the spirit. Jesus healed their sick because he was moved with compassion. Without compassion, a minister may treat the field as a gold mine instead of a flock scattered without a shepherd.

Obedience

The third requirement for successfully carrying out the work of God is obedience. Obedience is better than sacrifice. Obedience to the command of God is better than all the tithes one may pay. Again, to obey not to force the people of God to pay tithe is better than all so-called work of God that may be done with such tithe. First, Jesus commanded the disciples to feed the multitudes; they obeyed. Second he commanded them to bring the loaves of bread and fish; they obeyed. Ordinarily, five loaves cannot feed multitudes of five thousand men and innumerable women and children, but because the disciples obeyed the command of the Master, they were able to pull off that incredible project. They did not require some tithers or "financial pillars" to execute this project. The disciples learned this lesson, lived by it, and passed it on to us. Thus, what God requires from his children in respect of his command to go and make disciples of all nations, is to obey, not to collect tithes.

The Last Supper

Another project successfully executed in the days of the Lord was the Last Supper. The scriptures records as follows:

> Now on the first day of the Feast of Unleavened Bread the disciples came to Jesus, saying to Him, "Where do You want us to prepare for You to eat the Passover?" And He said, "Go into the city to a certain man, and say to him, 'The Teacher says, "My time is at hand; I will keep the Passover at your house with My disciples."' So the disciples did as Jesus had directed them; and they prepared the Passover. When evening had come, He sat down with the twelve (Matt 26:17–20).

"So the disciples did as Jesus had directed them." That is all that the contemporary church needs to do in respect of carrying the Great Commission or the work of God as it is generally referred to: "do as Jesus directed us." Did Jesus direct us to pay or collect tithes? Or did he direct us to give freely and generously? All that was necessary for this project to be successfully executed was "a certain man" who was willing to cheerfully sacrifice his house for the Lord to use for the Passover feast. He did not bring a tithe; he simply did as Jesus directed. He gave because he loved God. When we love God, we give as God gives those he loves.

GOD'S GIFT TO THE WORLD

How does God give? Are there lessons that today's Christian can learn from the way God gives gifts and blessings? The Bible is replete with records of God giving to his creatures. A couple of examples will suffice here:

> For God so loved the world that He gave His only begotten Son, that whoever believes in Him should not perish but have everlasting life (John 3:16).
> For even the Son of Man did not come to be served, but to serve, and to give His life a ransom for many (Mark 10:45).

who gave himself a ransom for all, to be testified in due
time (1 Tim 2:6).

God gives out of love. He gives freely. He gives willingly without compulsion. He gives generously. He gives his best. He gives with an altruistic purpose in mind. God has the salvation of man in mind when he gives. The church and individual Christians must learn to give just as God our father gives, not by compulsion but willingly.

Chapter 6

THE CHURCH'S ONE FOUNDATION

THE SCRIPTURES DECLARE THAT there is only one sure foundation, that is, Jesus Christ. The apostles and prophets were parts of this foundation and the (faith of the) Christian is built on this foundation:

> Now, therefore, you are no longer strangers and foreigners, but fellow citizens with the saints and members of the household of God, having been built on the foundation of the apostles and prophets, Jesus Christ Himself being the chief cornerstone (Eph 2:19–20).

If the Christian is built on this foundation which the apostles and prophets are part of, then, they should provide the Christian with examples of, and guidance to how to follow Christ and how to deal with every question of faith and related practices. In respect of tithing, the question the Christian should ask or answer is: "Did the apostles and prophets demand, collect or receive tithes?" If the answer is yes, then the Christian can follow their examples to demand, collect, and receive tithes. However, if the answer is no, then, the Christian must follow their example not to tithe. Even Paul the apostle enjoins the Christian to follow his example as he followed Christ (1 Cor 11:1).

Most of the New Testament was written by the apostle Paul. The teachings and traditions recorded in Paul's books set out the beliefs and praxis of the early church. Paul was quick to point out and condemn any contradiction of these beliefs and practices. For example, when the apostle Peter discriminated against Gentile brethren in Antioch for fear of the Jewish circumcision party who visited from Jerusalem, Paul confronted him openly and set things aright (Gal 2:11–16).

What Paul wrote and taught, he did after clear revelations of the mind of God. Where he gave relief and concession without the express command of God, he also clearly indicated so (I Cor 7:6). That was why he was very bold to challenge anyone who said or did anything contrary to these revealed truths. He did all that by the grace of God. That was why he boldly stated that "when James, Cephas, and John, who seemed to be pillars, perceived the grace that had been given to me, they gave me and Barnabas the right hand of fellowship, that we should go to the Gentiles and they to the circumcised" (Gal 2:9).

When the elders in Jerusalem gave Paul "the right hand of fellowship," that was to teach all that the Lord had revealed to him. They knew that the revelations did not include tithing, but they desire only one thing from Paul. According to Paul, "They desired only that we should remember the poor, the very thing which I also was eager to do" (Gal 2:10).

The teachings of Paul and his traditions serve as our light, as all the apostles agreed with him in their writings, and none of them expressed contrary opinions. Writing to the church, Paul said:

> Therefore I urge you, imitate me (1 Cor 4:16). Imitate me, just as I also imitate Christ (1 Cor 11:1). For you yourselves know how you ought to follow us, for we were not disorderly among you (2 Thess 3:7). You are witnesses, and God also, how devoutly and justly and blamelessly we behaved ourselves among you who believe; that you would walk worthy of God who calls you into His own kingdom and glory (1 Thess 2:10, 12). For this reason I have sent Timothy to you, who is my beloved and faithful son in the Lord, who will remind you of my ways in Christ, as I teach everywhere in every church (1 Cor 4:17). Now I praise you, brethren, that you remember

me in all things and keep the traditions just as I delivered them to you (1 Cor 11:2).

It was the practice of Paul to send his trusted fellow ministers to the churches to remind them what he had taught them so that they would not forget or get carried away by winds of doctrines that are erroneous. He urged the Christians of all eras and places to imitate him. That is to follow his teachings and traditions. What did he teach about tithe?

From all his letters, it could be seen clearly that Paul never taught nor practiced tithing. Paul mentioned tithes in very clear and unambiguous terms, and he did so in reference not to Christians, but to the Old Testament priests and Levites:

> And indeed those who are of the sons of Levi, who received the priesthood, have a commandment to receive tithes from the people according to the law, that is, from their brethren, though they have come from the loins of Abraham (Heb 7:5).

This was in respect of an express command to the Levites in the Old Testament to receive tithes from their brethren who were commanded to pay tithes to the sons of Levi. The Christian is not, anywhere, commanded to pay tithes to anyone. Moreover, this priesthood as discussed earlier was an imperfect priesthood instituted within an imperfect Old Testament, because as recorded in Hebrews 7:11, "if perfection were through the Levitical priesthood, what further need was there that another priest should rise according to the order of Melchizedek, and not be called according to the order of Aaron?" Hence, the need for it to be set aside and replaced by a better and perfect New Testament. Paul argued that since the Aaronic or Levitical priesthood was set aside and replaced by a better one, the law governing the priesthood was also changed:

> For the priesthood being changed, of necessity there is also a change of law. For on the one hand there is an annulling of the former commandment because of its weakness and unprofitableness, for the law made

nothing perfect; on the other hand, there is the bringing in of a better hope, through which we draw near to God (Heb 7:12, 18–19).

If the priesthood and the law governing it were changed or set aside, why should we continue to practice some aspects of the law just because it serves the material interests of some? We know that the payment of tithes was part of the old law that was set aside. As pointed out earlier, there is a difference between paying tithe and giving an offering.

Paul never taught that Christians should pay tithes but rather that we should give offerings. Paul further stated that all he did by his teaching on giving was to "give advice" (2 Cor 8:10) and not a commandment. Proponents of tithing have argued that "God commanded us to pay tithes and offering" but the word of God is clear as to how a Christian should give to God:

NOT BY COMMANDMENT

There is no commandment from God on how the Christian should give. That would have made giving a law and a duty, not a voluntary gift. In Second Corinthians 8:8, Paul explicitly declares "I speak not by commandment, but I am testing the sincerity of your love by the diligence of others." Christian giving is not a duty but a show of love for fellow believers and God. In other words, if a believer says that he loves God and the brethren, the sincerity of that love can be tested by the willingness of the believer to make sacrifices in the service of God and the brethren (see also Gal. 5:13–14). If it is by commandment then it is no longer for love, and God does not want us to worship him by force but willingly and out of love.

LIBERAL SHARING

Christian giving is a form of sharing. Those who have are enjoined to share with those in need. This giving is to meet the need of the ministers, saints, and all men (2 Cor 9:12–13) as already stated in the chapter dealing with the different types of tithes. Under the law of tithing, there were different types of tithes to meet the needs of various categories of citizens and inhabitants of the land. Likewise, in the New Testament, the offerings and gifts of the believers are meant to supply the needs of all categories of men particularly church members, not just only the ministers.

Paul went on to specify the criteria for the giving or offering that is pleasing and acceptable to God:

> Moreover, brethren, we make known to you the grace of God bestowed on the churches of Macedonia: that in a great trial of affliction the abundance of their joy and their deep poverty abounded in the riches of their liberality. For I bear witness that according to their ability, yes, and beyond their ability, they were freely willing, imploring us with much urgency that we would receive the gift and the fellowship of the ministering to the saints (2 Cor 8:1–4).
> For if there is first a willing mind, it is accepted according to what one has, and not according to what he does not have (2 Cor 8:12).
> Now concerning the ministering to the saints, it is superfluous for me to write to you; for I know your willingness, about which I boast of you to the Macedonians, that Achaia was ready a year ago; and your zeal has stirred up the majority. Therefore I thought it necessary to exhort the brethren to go to you ahead of time, and prepare your generous gift beforehand, which you had previously promised, that it may be ready as a matter of generosity and not as a grudging obligation. But this I say: He who sows sparingly will also reap sparingly, and he who sows bountifully will also reap bountifully. So let each one give as he purposes in his heart, not grudgingly or of necessity; for God loves a cheerful giver (2 Cor 9:1, 2, 5, 7).

Some words, clauses and phrases in the scriptures above express what the apostles taught about serving God generally, and in particular, giving to God in the New Testament. The gift of the churches of Macedonia was accepted because it met the criteria enumerated in the scriptures above. The following are some of the criteria:

GRACE OF GOD

The first thing we understand from the scriptures above is that the most important criterion for giving in the house of God is that we give by the grace of God. Giving or offering in the New Testament is by the grace of God. It is not by the command of the law. When we come to Christ, we do so by grace. When we are saved, we are saved by grace. When we work and labor in the house of God, we do so by grace. In the same vein, when we give gifts and offerings in the house of God, we do so by grace. Whatever we are or do, we are or do by grace.

GIVERS

Another thing we understand from the above scriptures is that those who finance the work of God are givers and not tithers. They are givers who give, not givers who tithe, nor tithers who give. What they give are gifts.

GIFT

When we give in the house of God, what we give is a gift not a payment. We cannot pay God for anything. We have to understand this. It is an insult to claim that we pay God. It is even a greater insult to claim that a child of God will perish in hell if he or she did not pay tithe. The offering we bring into the house of God that is acceptable to him is such as given willingly, freely, liberally, joyfully and according to ability. It must also be a generous gift.

GENEROSITY

Generosity is a logical manifestation of the grace of God in the life of a Christian. When Christians give to God, they must give generously because God our father taught us by giving generously, and his grace enables us to do so. Moreover, he who sows sparingly will also reap sparingly, and he who sows bountifully will also reap bountifully.

FELLOWSHIP

Fellowship means doing things together or sharing. It is not one person doing something for which others pay. When we give our offerings we are sharing what God has blessed us with, not only with the ministers of the gospel but all the house of God. We are not paying for the work of the ministry which ministers do because freely they received and freely they are commanded to give (Matthew 10:8). Just as the ministers freely received and are commanded to freely give of the benefits of the gospel, the believers are enjoined to share their material things freely, willingly, liberally, joyfully, and according to ability.

MINISTERING TO THE SAINTS

To minister is to serve. Ministering to the saints is serving the saints or rendering service to the saints. Showing hospitality, hosting the brethren, caring for the sick, feeding the hungry, and sending relief materials are examples of ministering to the saints. Our giving in the church is the fellowship of the ministering to the saints. We have noted that fellowship is sharing. Thus, giving is sharing or taking part in serving the saints. When we give money or material things for the benefit of the people of God, we are sharing or participating in ministering to the saints. Ministering to the saints is only acceptable to God if we do it freely, willingly, liberally, joyfully, and according to ability. This is possible by the grace of God.

PROMISE

It is a promise. As pointed out earlier, a promise is voluntary. You may not be obligated to do something, but you can promise to do it. A vow is a promise made with an oath. For example, Jacob made such a promise to God when he was running away from his brother Esau. God did not demand him to build a house at Bethel for him, but Jacob chose to, and promised to do so.

JOY

The giving that is acceptable to God is that which is done with joy, not with sadness. The churches of Macedonia gave not just with joy but abundance of their joy. That they gave with joy means that they counted it a privilege to give to God. That was why they implored Paul and his team with much persuasion to receive their gift and were abundantly joyful when they gave. That can only be by the grace of God.

LIBERALITY

The giving that is acceptable to God is one done liberally, not sparingly. Stinginess is a state of the mind and it is not commendable in God's sight. I feel it was stinginess of the children of Israel that made God to institute tithing in the law. In Christ, a believer's heart is purged of stinginess. Hence, we give liberally. Even if a believer is poor, when he gives liberally, the little he gives is regarded as rich in the sight of God. Our giving is the liberality of the people of God who even in their deep poverty—like the poor widow that gave her mites—give in rich liberality. Liberality is an outcome of the grace of God.

ACCORDING TO ABILITY

God expect us to give to him according to our ability, that is, what we are able to give, and not what we are unable to give. When preachers put pressure on their congregations to give more than is within their capacity, they force them to give not according to their ability. God is not impressed that you used your children's school fees to "sow seed" in the hope that God would give you a hundred-fold in return because that is not giving according to your ability. The giving that is acceptable to God is that which is according to one's ability. Similarly, we are to give according to what we have.

ACCORDING TO WHAT ONE HAS

An important feature of the offering that God accepts is that it is according to what one has and not according to what he does not have. God is not expecting from one if one has nothing to give. Actually, in the Old Testament, the tithe for the poor was meant to cater for such person. There are many ways one can give to God apart from money. One can give one's time, services, and other non-monetary offerings. However, one has to give according to what one has. When preachers cajole and pressurize members of their congregations to give of what they did not have, such as their children's school fees, that is robbery and God does not accept such.

AS ONE PURPOSES IN ONE'S HEART

The offering that pleases God is that which is given as one purposes in one's heart, or chooses or plans to give. It could be ten percent of one's income, less or more. It could be in cash or kind but it must be as one purposed in one's heart, not as dictated by some law or preachers. Once a specific amount is imposed, it is no longer as one purposes in one's heart but as prescribed by a law.

FREELY

Giving to God is only acceptable when done freely and not by compulsion. God is not impressed with your huge donations if not freely given because if you are forced to give up a possession, that would be robbery. God cannot, and does not rob us. However, by his grace we can give joyfully, liberally, and according to our ability.

WILLINGNESS

Our offering must not only be freely given but also we must give willingly. God accepts our offerings when we give from a willing heart. A willing gift is given freely, according to ability, liberally, and joyfully. This willingness is possible by the grace of God.

ZEAL

Zeal is the opposite of being lukewarm. Titus (2:14) says that Christ redeemed and purified "His own special people, zealous for good works." This means that as Christians we ought to serve God with zeal and not be lukewarm in his service. Thus, the offering that God accepts is one given zealously. If we are lukewarm and not eager or enthusiastic to give to God, then our offering may not be acceptable to him irrespective of the amount we give. God looks at the heart of the giver and he can see whether the giver is zealous about giving or lukewarm. A zealous giver is also a cheerful giver.

CHEERFUL GIVER

God loves a cheerful giver. A cheerful giver does not give just because he is pressurized to give, neither does he feel compelled to do so when he gives. He gives willingly, freely, liberally, joyfully, zealously, generously, according to ability, and as he purposes in his heart. A cheerful giver does not give grudgingly. Unfortunately, many people who pay tithes today do so grudgingly.

NOT AS A GRUDGING OBLIGATION

When we give to God, we ought to give cheerfully and not grudgingly because giving grudgingly is tantamount to accusing God of forcing us to give up our possession, or robbing us of our possessions. People give grudgingly if they see giving as an obligation or compulsory duty—payment—rather than a joyful gratitude. God does not delight in grudging obligations. Rather he desires that we approach him in grateful appreciation of his mercy which we received by grace. An obligation is something that must be done or observed necessarily. This seems more like tithe which is a necessary payment.

NOT OF NECESSITY

What Christians give in the house of God is not a necessity. First, it is not a necessity for the work of God because the work of God can be accomplished, and is always accomplished without the obligatory intervention of men as God always provides for his work. Second, it is not a necessity for blessings or prosperity as God's blessings, and material prosperity in particular, are free and cannot be purchased by paying any amount. Third, it is not a necessity for salvation as we are not saved by what we give or pay, but by what we receive through grace when we repent.

JUST, PURE AND UNBLEMISHED

The gift that is acceptable to God must be pure, unblemished, and of a just and righteous source. God does not accept the proceeds of injustice and wickedness. God warns, "I, the LORD, love justice; I hate robbery for burnt offering" (Isa 61:8). You cannot disobey God by robbing others and make sacrifices of huge offerings. God hates such. That is why he says that obedience is better than sacrifice. Whether the giver is robbed or the giver is the one robbing others to give, God does not accept such. Your pastor may accept a tithe of the proceed of scam, fraud, corruption, prostitution, drug peddling, robbery, bribery, cheating, oppression, extortion, and any such wickedness, but such is not acceptable to God. It is not compulsory that we give to God. It is better we do not give at all than to give what is condemnable before God. Thus, whenever we give, we must give that which is acceptable and pleasing to him.

As has been stated over and again, when we bring our offerings to God, it is only a gift, not a payment. We give to God because we love him, not because we are afraid that he would curse us. When you love somebody, you give that person gifts. God taught us how to give by giving us his son Jesus Christ (John 3:16). So we reciprocate by giving and not by paying. Tithing as practiced in the church today is a payment. We should not dare bring a payment before God because we cannot pay him for any of his blessings. We cannot afford the price, so he paid the price in Christ and gave him to us as a gift.

However, if a Christian decides or vows to bring a gift of the tenth of his income to the house of the Lord, then that is his personal choice, which is not, and should not be binding on any other person. He can also decide to stop bringing a tenth and bring something less or more than the tenth as he chooses. It is between that particular Christian and God, and God blesses him according to his heart's disposition and not according to what he brings. If somebody gives plenty but out of a proud heart or grudgingly, he does not get any blessing because he insults God, and may attract the wrath of God who loves a cheerful giver. A good example is the story of Ananias and Sapphira (Acts 5:1–10).

On the other hand, if someone gives joyfully and cheerfully, even if what is given is a small token, God is happy with that person and blesses him abundantly. God just wants us to serve him freely out of a cheerful, and willing heart without burdens and encumbrances. Whatever we do for God, he wants us to do it willingly and not by compulsion. God, through Apostle Peter, expressly urges the ministers of the gospel to "Shepherd the flock of God which is among you, serving as overseers, not by compulsion but willingly, not for dishonest gain but eagerly; nor as being lords over those entrusted to you, but being examples to the flock" (1 Pet 5:2–3).

This is exactly the same thing that Paul emphasized. All the apostles and Bible writers agree on these issues. However, Paul did not overlook the fact that the minister of the gospel requires the support of the church to carry on the work of God. This is his assertion on the command of the Lord as to how a minister of the gospel should earn his living:

> Do you not know that those who minister the holy things eat of the things of the temple, and those who serve at the altar partake of the offerings of the altar? Even so the Lord has commanded that those who preach the gospel should live from the gospel (1 Cor 9:13–14).

Thus, the word of God commands the believers to support and sustain the ministers of the gospel in this manner: "Let him who is taught the word share in all good things with him who teaches" (Gal 6:6).

Those who preach the gospel should live from the gospel, not from the altar. These are two different things. The altar was of the Old Testament while the gospel is of the New Testament. The altar was stationary whereas the gospel is mobile. The altar was attended to by a tribe of non-working, non-propertied and dependent priests, whereas the gospel is preached by all believers who both work and own properties. The priests who attended to the altar were paid tithes while the ministers of the gospel live from the gifts that the brethren willingly, cheerfully, joyfully, voluntarily and generously give.

Paul was a preacher who did not keep from the church anything that would be a blessing to them. If tithes were acceptable in the New Testament, Paul would have taught it and practiced it in an unambiguous manner. How he handled the issues of circumcision, marriage, the position of women in the church, the love and respect of women in the home, and genealogies is insightful. His position and practices concerning giving in the church have been the main subjects of this section. He never minced words about anything that pertained to the edification and blessing of the church. Why did Paul not teach about tithe the same way he taught about gifts? If tithe was as important as present-day ministers would want us to believe, why did Paul leave such an important issue to guesswork and inferences based on the Old Testament requirements?

To clearly disassociate himself from the demands of the law such as tithe, Paul spoke extensively about gifts and also claimed his right to such gifts as a minister of the gospel and an apostle of Jesus Christ. However, Paul did not abuse his right to these gifts. In fact, he refused to use this right to these legitimate gifts just because he did not want the work of the gospel to be hindered. He worked with his own hands to provide for himself. In First Corinthians 9:4, 6, 11-12 Paul reminded the church of his right in the gospel and also explained why he had not used that right:

> Do we have no right to eat and drink? Or is it only Barnabas and I who have no right to refrain from working? If we have sown spiritual things for you, is it a great thing if we reap your material things? If others are partakers of this right over you, are we not even more? Nevertheless, we have not used this right, but endure all things lest we hinder the gospel of Christ.

The tone of Paul in these verses did not sound like he was telling this church what they must do to avert the curse of God and "a rampaging devourer." He sounded rather like arguing with the church over their doubt about Paul's apostleship because he was not depending on their freely given material supplies. Then he assertively told them that he was their own apostle. "If I am not an apostle to others, yet doubtless I am to you. For you are the seal of my apostleship in the Lord" (verse 2). That apostleship goes with a right but Paul did not enforce that right, rather he said "I have used none of these things, nor have I written these things that it should be done so to me; for it would be better for me to die than that anyone should make my boasting void" (verse 15).

If this right were a compulsory thing, Paul would not have had any option but to use it, otherwise, he would be condemning the people to severe adverse consequences. But we know that Paul would never do such a thing as to endanger the spiritual welfare of the converts he jeopardized his own life to win for the Lord. Thus, Paul was not referring to tithe in these scriptures. Rather, he was referring to freewill gifts, which were received with many commendations. Read Paul in Philippians 4:10–18:

> But I rejoice in the Lord greatly that now at last your care for me has flourished again; though you surely did care, but you lacked opportunity. Not that I speak in regard to need, for I have learned in whatever state I am, to be content: I know how to be abased, and I know how to abound. Everywhere and in all things I have learned both to be full and to be hungry, both to abound and to suffer need. I can do all things through Christ who strengthens me. Nevertheless you have done well that you shared in my distress. Now you Philippians know also that in the beginning of the gospel, when I departed from Macedonia, no church shared with me concerning giving and receiving but you only. For even in Thessalonica you sent aid once and again for my necessities. Not that I seek the gift, but I seek the fruit that abounds to your account. Indeed I have all and abound. I am full, having received from Epaphroditus the things sent from you, a sweet-smelling aroma, an acceptable sacrifice, well pleasing to God.

This portion of the scriptures is very self-explanatory. This is an example by the great apostle that we should follow, an example that contemporary preachers should follow. He talked about his needs and necessities in which as we have seen earlier, that he did not want to make himself a burden of the church. He learned to be content in whatever situation he was. However, the Philippi church chose to share with him. They were not under obligation to send a "tithe" to Paul. The other churches did not send anything to Paul because they were not bound to do so. If they were paying tithes in those days, Paul would never have been in need because he would have been receiving their regular mandatory tithes.

DID CHRISTIANS PAY TITHES FROM THE BEGINNING OF THE CHURCH?

Contemporary tithe preachers tell us that the church had always paid tithes. This is not the Bible truth. Paul said in Philippians 4:15 that "in the beginning of the gospel," the churches "shared" their "generousity." They did not pay tithes. The words are "share" and "generousity" not "pay" or "tithe." Thus, tithing was not one of the practices of the early church, it was introduced some centuries down the line. Even after tithing was introduced in the 6th Century, it was not made compulsory.[1]

According to Constable:

> Very little is known about the actual payment of tithes in the first centuries of Christianity. Their early history is a subject . . . 'on the details of which learned authorities will probably forever disagree'. 'The faithful may have paid the tithe voluntarily and spontaneously,' according to Leclercq, 'but we are not in a position to cite any canonical or conciliar text before the fourth century which requires the payment [of tithes].[2]

If tithing was not practiced in the early church, how did it become a Christian doctrine? Fanning in the Catholic Encyclopedia records that:

> In the Christian Church, as those who serve the altar should live by the altar (1Corinthians 9:13), provision of some kind had necessarily to be made for the sacred ministers. In the beginning this was supplied by the spontaneous offerings of the faithful. In the course of time, however, as the Church expanded and various institutions arose, it became necessary to make laws which would insure the proper and permanent support of the clergy. The payment of tithes was adopted from the Old Law, and early writers speak of it as a divine ordinance and obligation of conscience. The earliest positive legislation on the subject seems to be contained in the letter

1. Constable, *Monastic Tithes*.

2. Constable, *Monastic Tithes*, 19.

of Bishops assembled at Tours in 567 and the canons of the Council of Macon in 585. In course of time, we find the payment of tithes made obligatory by ecclesiastical enactments in all countries of Christendom.[3]

The fact needs not be over-flogged anymore that tithing was not part of Christian worship from the beginning. The payment of tithes became part of Christian worship almost six hundred years later by man-made laws, and it was not compulsory at this point in time. The historical evidence provided above shows how tithing found its way into the New Testament Church. Furthermore, when tithing was introduced in the 6th Century Roman Catholic Church, everybody, priests and laity alike, were obligated to pay tithes without exceptions:

> All men, therefore, whatever their position in the Church, had to pay tithes. Like prayer, charity, and the Ten Commandments, it was a personal religious obligation from which there could be no exemptions . . . And the act of rendering tithes, as Schreiber said, took on 'a certain liturgical character' and was treated as 'an act of worshipping God'.[4]

Actually, the doctrine of tithing as a necessary condition for salvation of the soul was a Roman Catholic propagation. According to Constable:

> For tithes are paid, according to St Caesar of Arles in a sermon universally attributed to St Augustine in the Middle Ages, for the sake not of God who receives them but of those who pay them, whose eternal salvation depends upon faithful payment.[5]

Thus, the church from this time began to teach, though without scriptural authority, that "Tithe is a due . . . which must, at the

3. Fanning, *Tithes.*
4. Constable, *Monastic Tithes*, 15.
5. Constable, *Monastic Tithes*, 13.

risk of his soul, be paid by every believer."[6] This is indeed contrary to the teachings and practices of the apostles and the early church.

In the days of the apostles and the First Century church, there was no payment of tithes. Paul and other apostles never demanded nor accepted payment for the work of the gospel but they accepted freewill gifts from the church. If the church did not pay tithes from the beginning of the gospel, why should we pay tithes now?

6. Constable, *Monastic Tithes*, 15.

Chapter 7

THE CONVERGENCE OF CHRIST AND MELCHIZEDEK

THE LEVITICAL PRIESTHOOD HAS been compared with the priesthood of the Lord Jesus Christ and it has been seen how they diverge on many points. This is because the priesthood of Jesus Christ is not according to the order of Aaron but according to the order of Melchizedek. A closer look at the priesthood of Jesus and the priesthood of Melchizedek shows a lot of convergence, which gives much light on the issue of tithing. The dispensation of the priesthood of Melchizedek was before the law while the dispensation of the priesthood of the Lord Jesus Christ brought an end to the law. Thus, this order of priesthood was outside the law. The priesthood of Aaron, therefore, was a legalistic dispensation, which served as tutelage for the people of Israel who had lost touch with the true worship of God.

Apart from the issue of tithe, there were other issues like faith, grace, meekness, forgiveness, and mercy, which at the time the law was given, had become almost forgotten by the children of Israel. For example, Moses permitted the people to divorce their spouses because of the hardness of their hearts (Mark 10:4–5). They could not forgive. Rebellion against Moses and God was rampant because they lacked faith. They complained and rebelled for everything.

When they cried for food, God sent them manner (Exod 16:1–4), yet they did not believe him to give them water (Exod 17:1–3). They have forgotten the faith of Abraham, the grace of Isaac, the meekness of Jacob, and the forgiveness and mercy of Joseph.

So God had to give the law as a guide to enforce a similitude of God's standard for every aspect of their relationship and to lead them to Christ. As the scriptures record:

> But before faith came, we were kept under guard by the law, kept for the faith which would afterward be revealed. Therefore, the law was our tutor to bring us to Christ, that we might be justified by faith. But after faith has come, we are no longer under a tutor (Gal 3:23–25).

"We were kept under guard by the law" in a forced relationship which is not what God wants with us. A voluntary relationship was what he had with Abel, Enoch, Noah, Abraham, Isaac, Jacob, and Moses before the law was given. This was the era of the priesthood of Melchizedek. But why was the law needed in the first place if it was not the perfect covenant? Galatians 3:19 gives the purpose which the law served: "It was added because of transgressions, till the Seed should come to whom the promise was made." God saw the heart of the people of Israel, that they would not willingly support the priests and Levites (that was the transgression), and therefore commanded tithing as part of the Old Testament law. It was this kind of heart of transgression that made God rebuke them in Malachi chapter three.

If we in the New Testament still require a commandment to support the work of our father, then, we are not doing it willingly, freely, liberally, joyfully, cheerfully, zealously, generously, sacrificially, according to ability, and as we purpose in our heart. Thus we are still living in transgression. We are still living under the law in the Old Testament and have not known the Christ that transforms the hearts of men. When the Lord Jesus came, he fulfilled the requirements of the law: the tutor, and set it aside and brought us back to the priesthood in the order of Melchizedek. Let us see a few points on which the priesthood of Christ is similar to that of Melchizedek.

ABSENCE OF THE LAW

The absence of the law is common to the two dispensations. Until the coming of the law, people did not worship God according to law neither were they saved by the work of the law but by faith. They pleased God by faith for the Bible says that it is impossible to please God without faith (Heb 11:6). Furthermore, Hebrews chapter 11 emphasized the centrality of faith:

> By faith Abel offered to God a more excellent sacrifice than Cain, through which he obtained witness that he was righteous, God testifying of his gifts; and through it he being dead still speaks. By faith Enoch was taken away so that he did not see death, and was not found, because God has taken him, for before he was taken he had this testimony, that he pleased God.
>
> By faith Noah, being divinely warned of things not yet seen, moved with godly fear, prepared an ark for the saving of his household, by which he condemned the world and became heir of the righteousness which is according to faith. By faith Abraham obeyed when he was called to go out to the place which he would receive as an inheritance. And he went out, not knowing where he was going.
>
> By faith Isaac blessed Jacob and Esau concerning things to come. By faith Jacob, when he was dying, blessed each of the sons of Joseph, and worshiped, leaning on top of his staff. By faith Joseph, when he was dying, made mention of the departure of the children of Israel, and gave instructions concerning his bones.
>
> By faith Moses, when he became of age, refused to be called the son of Pharaoh's daughter, choosing rather to suffer affliction with the people of God than to enjoy the passing pleasures of sin (Heb 11:4–5, 7–8, 20–22, 24–25).

Reading through Hebrews chapter 11, you see men and women who walked with God and did exploit by faith and not by the law. Take Moses for instance; no law commanded him to defy Pharaoh and his daughter by refusing to be called the son of Pharaoh's daughter. No law required that he suffer affliction with

sow nothing and if you sow nothing you reap nothing. This is the law of sowing and reaping. When a farmer plants his seeds he harvests the fruits during the harvest time.

A farmer may sow his seeds but not reap commensurately or he may not reap at all if the necessary conditions are not available. If the soil is not fertile, the farmer may plant a seed but not reap a commensurate amount of harvest. If the rains did not come at the appropriate time, or if the rains did not come at all, the farmer may not reap as he should. This is the case with those who sow natural seeds. Nothing is certain in the natural world. But in the spiritual realm, everything is certain. If you sow, you reap. The soil is certainly fertile, the rains certainly come and in due season. As you sow, so you reap. If you sow sparingly you reap sparingly. If you sow bountifully you reap bountifully.

When you give you gain. God gave us his son and he gained us as his children. By so doing he set for us an example on how to give, and taught us that "it is more blessed to give than to receive" (Acts 20:35). When you give, what you give is returned to you in a measure that there will not be enough room to accommodate them (Mal 3:10). You give a measure, you gain good measure. You give scattering, you gain them pressed down shaken together. You give out of a drying source, you gain them running over. You give with the hand, you gain them put in your bosom, that is, your hands, chest, and lap. Measure here refers to proportion or percentage. There is no commanded specific measure, proportion, or percentage of income that a Christian must give, rather a believer is advised to decide what percentage of his income to offer. One widow chose to give all her livelihood which amounted to two mites or a quadrans. God is pleased with and blesses what one chooses to give, not what one is forced to give. Giving bountifully or sparingly depends on the measure one gives, not the amount. Thus, the poor in the church often give more than the rich because they often give a higher proportion of their income while the rich give a larger amount but very little proportion of their income. The same measure you give is the measure you gain but now in good measure, pressed down, shaken together, and running over. That is what God can do for you when you give willingly, freely, liberally, joyfully, cheerfully, zealously, generously, sacrificially, according to ability, and as you purpose in your heart. This is the kind of giving that God respects, not the compulsory legal obligation that contemporary preachers, contrary to scriptures, charge in the name of tithing.

Chapter 8

The Curse

Proponents of New Testament tithing have told us that those who do not pay tithe are cursed with a curse. Is that the Bible truth? Let us allow the Bible to speak for itself here. The curse in question here is pronounced in Malachi 3:9. To whom was this often threatened curse directed? Let us seek answers from the man that delivered the message with the curse: the prophet Malachi.

The prophet began his prophecy by clearly stating that the burden or vision God gave him was to Israel (Mal 1:1), that means that his vision was not to the Gentiles. In case contemporary preachers of tithing are in doubt of which Israel God was referring to, the second verse of Malachi chapter one emphasized that it was the brother of Esau. "Was not Esau Jacob's brother?" God asked them. Thus, the Israel being referred to in Malachi was the same Jacob, the brother of Esau. Jacob later became Israel and a nation. It was to this nation that God gave the priesthood and priests to mediate between him and them.

Chapter two of Malachi starts with "And now, O priests." God was talking to his priests, not Gentile priests. They were priests of Israel. In verse 11 of the same chapter, God emphasized that his message to Malachi was for Judah, and again it was not for Gentiles. Judah "has dealt treacherously" and God was not happy.

Chapter three began by God saying that "I send My messenger, and he will prepare the way before Me. And the Lord, whom you seek, will suddenly come to His temple" (verse 1). Who were the people seeking the Lord, and to whom did the Lord of hosts send his messenger? Was is to Israelites or Gentiles? Of course the answer is Israelites. It took another four hundred years before the Lord, whom they sought, came suddenly to his temple in Jerusalem, Judah, in Israel. Verse three of that chapter gives a clearer understanding of those to whom Malachi was sent to. It reads thus:

> He will sit as a refiner and a purifier of silver; He will purify the sons of Levi, and purge them as gold and silver, that they may offer to the LORD an offering in righteousness.

Why did God want the sons of Levi to offer an offering in righteousness? The answer is provided in the following verse: "Then the offering of Judah and Jerusalem will be pleasant to the LORD" (Mal 3:4). God emphasized the centrality of the offices of the sons of Levi, namely, the priests and Levites in the worship of God by Israelites. The sons of Levi were the mediators of the Old Covenant. Therefore, they must be purged, clean and pure in order to do their work in righteousness. Their work was to make offering to God on behalf of Jerusalem, Judah, and entire Israel. Thus, if they offer to the Lord in righteousness, then "the offering of Judah and Jerusalem will be pleasant to the LORD." Conversely, if they offer it in unrighteousness, the offering of Judah and Jerusalem, that is, Israel, will not be pleasant to the Lord. In other words, God was more pleased by their righteousness than what they were offering because it was their righteousness that made their offering pleasant to him. At the time Malachi was delivering his message, they had gone away from God's ordinances and have not kept them (Mal 1:6–8, 12–14, 2:8, 10–12). Therefore, God had no pleasure in them, and would not accept their offering (Mal 1:10). Rather God made them contemptible and base, and did not regard their offering anymore (Mal 2:9, 13).

Now, to these people pertained the ordinances of tithes and offerings of Malachi 3:8–10, the favorite scriptures of contemporary proponents of tithing. These verses are often cited as infallible authority on tithing, and the foundation upon which they build their doctrines on the subject.

When God said "you have robbed Me! . . . In tithes and offerings. You are cursed with a curse," who was he referring to? When he commanded them to "Bring all the tithes into the storehouse," who was he commanding? Was he commanding Israel or the church? Of course he was commanding the nation of Israel "Even this whole nation," and not the church. The church does not have storehouses; the nation of Israel did. Furthermore, the church is not under the law; the nation of Israel was. The word of God says:

> Now we know that whatever the law says, it says to those
> who are under the law, that every mouth may be stopped,
> and all the world may become guilty before God (Rom
> 3:19).

Thus, the law was meant for the nation of Israel and not the church. Furthermore, the law which includes tithing is good, profitable, and effective only if used lawfully:

> we know that the law is good if one uses it lawfully,
> knowing this: that the law is not made for a righteous
> person, but for the lawless and insubordinate, for the
> ungodly and for sinners (1 Tim 1:8–9).

"Lawfully" here means "within the context." Thus, using the law lawfully means operating the law within the context of the law, that is, within the context of lawlessness, insubordination, ungodliness, and sin. Operating the law outside the context of the law renders it unprofitable and ineffective. Knowing this, Paul rebuked the Galatian church for yielding to pressure to incorporate the law into their Christian faith. He chided them:

> O foolish Galatians! Who has bewitched you that you
> should not obey the truth, before whose eyes Jesus Christ
> was clearly portrayed among you as crucified? This only
> I want to learn from you: Did you receive the Spirit by

the work of the law, or by the hearing of faith? Are you so foolish? Having begun in the Spirit, are you now being made perfect by the flesh? Therefore He who supplies the Spirit to you and works miracles among you, does He do it by the works of the law, or by the hearing of faith? (Gal 3:1–3, 5).

Furthermore, Galatians 3:6–9 emphasizes the blessedness of righteousness, the righteousness that is of faith, the righteousness which Abraham received by faith, and this faith the scriptures say was in the gospel which was preached to Abraham. The gospel, not the law was preached to Abraham. Thus, the tithe Abraham gave was a freewill gift or "sharing" which is in accordance with the gospel, not the Levitical tithe which was according to the law. The scriptures declare that:

> just as Abraham "believed God, and it was accounted to him for righteousness." Therefore know that only those who are of faith are sons of Abraham. And the scripture, foreseeing that God would justify the Gentiles by faith, preached the gospel to Abraham beforehand, saying, "In you all the nations shall be blessed." So then those who are of faith are blessed with believing Abraham.

If only those who are of faith are sons of Abraham and are blessed with Abraham, who then are cursed with a curse? Again the Bible in Galatians 3:10–12 has the answer to that question:

> For as many as are of the works of the law are under the curse; for it is written, "Cursed is everyone who does not continue in all things which are written in the book of the law, to do them." But that no one is justified by the law in the sight of God is evident, for "the just shall live by faith." Yet the law is not of faith, but "the man who does them shall live by them."

From these scriptures, it is evident that those who are under the curse are Christians who live by the law, one aspect of which is obligatory tithing. Those who live by the law must fulfill all its requirements, such as the observance of Sabbath day and circumcision. The "man who does them shall live by them," but he cannot pick and choose what aspect of the law to keep and which aspect to neglect. He must "continue," in other words, never stop doing, but fulfil "all things which are written in the book of the law." However, while doing all that is written in the law, he must also bear in mind "that no one is justified by the law in the sight of God . . . for the just shall live by faith." Thus, the believer's justification and inheritance in Christ is only by faith:

> For the promise that he would be the heir of the world was not to Abraham or to his seed through the law, but through the righteousness of faith. For if those who are of the law are heirs, faith is made void and the promise made of no effect (Rom 4:13–14).

Therefore, those who teach that obligatory tithing in the New Testament is commanded by God, and those who pay tithe with the mindset of fulfilling the law, should endeavor to continue in all that is written in the book of the law, for the consequences of not doing so is clearly spelled out in the scriptures.

Again, Christians have been told that they have to pay tithe so there may be food in God's house. The questions that arise here are: "Does God really need assistance from us to feed his house?" "Does God need anything from us?" "Does God need anything from anyone?" "What does God want from his children?" This is God's answer to these questions:

> If I were hungry, I would not tell you; For the world is Mine, and all its fullness.
> Offer to God thanksgiving, And pay your vows to the Most High. Call upon Me in the day of trouble; I will deliver you, and you shall glorify Me (Ps 50:12, 14–15).

God needs nothing from us. What we bring to God is a token of our appreciation for what he has done for us and what he has given us in Christ Jesus. It is our show of love (2 Cor 8:8) and thanksgiving, not our duties or payment for the blessings of God. Neither is it a down payment for a hundredfold material reward. God imposes no charges on us. He only requires us to "offer" thanksgiving and "pay" or fulfill the vows we made to him. If we vow to do something for God, then it is voluntary. In the New Testament, the apostles did not teach or practice tithing. Rather they encouraged voluntary sharing and giving, which they received with much gratitude and commendation (Phil 4:10–18). It was never a mandatory duty.

Luke 16:16 says, "The law and the prophets were until John. Since that time the kingdom of God has been preached." Until John the Baptist, the law and all its traditions and duties including tithing held sway but with the advent of John who was the forerunner of the Lord Jesus Christ, the kingdom of God began to be preached up to now. How did the Lord say we must get into the kingdom? How is the kingdom preached? This is how: "The time is fulfilled, and the kingdom of God is at hand, repent, and believe in the gospel" (Mark1:15). Repent and believe. This speaks about having faith unto salvation, not making payments for salvation. The kingdom of God is about faith, cheerful, and willing service. Whatever is not of faith is sin (Rom 14:23).

Faith has always been the requirement for walking with God. Abel made an acceptable sacrifice by faith. Enoch walked with God and God took him that he did not see death. How did he walk with God? By faith! Noah believed God's warning concerning the flood and he and his household were saved. Abraham believed the promises of God and it was counted for him for righteousness. He was willing to sacrifice Isaac his son believing that God who asked him to do so would raise his son back to life. These happened before the law.

Under the law, those who did exploit were those who exceeded the requirement of the law and thereby lived above the law. Moses, Joshua, Gideon, David, and innumerable others who achieved exceptional feats did not achieve such feats by the law, they did so by believing God. After the law was set aside, in the New Testament, the fullness of faith was revealed. Anyone who is saved is saved by faith. So whether before the law, under the law or after the law, walking with God and maintaining a relationship with him is on the basis of grace received by faith. Thus, our service or offering to God is a token of our appreciation for God's grace and goodness to us. It is never a payment for what God has done or what he is going to do for us. God does not want us to pay, because we cannot afford the price of his blessings or redemption. He gave it to us free. So when we bring an offering to him, we should see it as exactly what it is: a freewill gift out of what God has blessed us with. Thus, we must give cheerfully and generously. However, we must never tremble with guilt and condemnation before God if we did not have to give, and therefore did not bring anything. God delights in our cheerful giving and gratitude not condemnation.

When we feel guilty for not paying tithe because we have been told that we are robbing God, that insults God because that means telling God that we are worried that we owe him part payment for our redemption and his numerous blessings. God is our father and we owe him nothing but thanksgiving and holy living. Just like our natural fathers, we do not tremble before them because we did not bring a specified portion of our income as payment for being born by them. On the contrary, it is the joy of parents to provide their children with all life's necessities such as food, clothing, and education. In return, we thank them for what they did for us. When we earn incomes, it is not mandatory that we give our natural parents a particular portion of our incomes, but we decide what we give them, and willingly and joyfully too. Likewise, what we give to God is our willing and joyful thanksgiving and not a payment enforced by law.

Abraham gave a tithe to Melchizedek willingly. It was not because a law commanded him to do so. Likewise, no law commands the Christian to pay tithe because Christ is a priest in the order of Melchizedek not in the order of Aaron. The problem with the doctrine of tithing in the New Testament is that preachers use the Aaronic priesthood to explain the priesthood of Melchizedek. The Holy Spirit inspired the author of Hebrews to carefully choose his words to reflect the true nature of tithe in respect of the Levitical priesthood. In Hebrews 7:2, 4, 5, 9 he said, Abraham "gave" a tenth to Melchizedek. On the other hand, Levi "paid." Abraham was not commanded to give a tithe to Melchizedek, he chose to. On the other hand, Levi was commanded by law to take a tithe from his brethren. Thus, Abraham's tithe was of faith while Levi's tithe was of the law, the law that was made for the unrighteous transgressors. The Christian is of faith not of the law. Hence, the Christian is under no commandment to pay tithe. He can choose to give a tenth or more or less of his income. It is his choice and not an imposition of the law.

If we accept that the Christian should pay tithe to Christ our High Priest, then we must also accept that they should bring the tithe to Christ himself physically as Abraham did to Melchizedek. Otherwise, those who take tithes have arrogated to themselves the position of Christ, which is the office of our High Priest who attends to the altar in heaven. On the other hand, if we accept that all of us are members of Christ on earth, then either we are all entitled to the tithe or we are not commanded to take tithe. The Christians, especially the rich ones are commanded to share willingly, they were not commanded to tithe willy-nilly.

When it comes to work of God like evangelizing the world, building church houses, buying vehicles for the church, feeding the poor, and the like, God usually provides for himself "a lamb for the sacrifice." God usually provides for himself the resources for his work and does not depend on tithes for such projects.

Under the law, the priest and Levites were commanded to take tithes from their brethren because they were not permitted to work or have a share of the land like the other tribes of Israel. The scriptures say that the dispensation of the Old Testament priesthood has been changed. Likewise, the law also was changed with its traditions and duties. In the New Testament, the ministers are free to work as Paul did. Even if gospel ministers are on full time, their remunerations should be according to scriptural prescriptions. Furthermore, where churches truly use tithes for the work of God, they are not under any scriptural authority to collect tithes as a mandatory and legally binding payment from believers.

In the light of the above, when a preacher frightens and threatens his congregation with "you are cursed with a curse" to get them to pay tithe, it is tantamount to extortion. The scripture is clear on how to relate with extortioners. You might have condoned them hitherto, "But now I have written to you not to keep company with anyone named a brother, who is sexually immoral, or covetous, or an idolater, or a reviler, or a drunkard, or an extortioner— not even to eat with such a person" (1 Cor 5:11).

From the foregoing, it is clear that tithing in the New Testament is not mandatory. Thus ministers of the gospel should stop holding the church of Jesus Christ hostage by threatening them with "you are cursed with a curse" if they did not "pay" tithes. There is no curse against a Christian for "Christ has redeemed us from the curse of the law, having become a curse for us . . . that the blessings of Abraham might come upon the Gentiles in Christ Jesus" (Gal 3:13–14). Having stated that, under certain circumstances, an individual believer may give a tithe of his or her income. The following chapter discusses those conditions.

Chapter 9

THE COMMISSION
AND CONSECRATION

AN INDIVIDUAL CHRISTIAN BELIEVER may be permitted to give a tithe of his or her income as a freewill offering if any of the following conditions is fulfilled:

SPIRIT'S COMMISSION

If one justifies the payment of tithe by citing Malachi 3:8–10, then, one brings oneself under the law. "But if you are led by the Spirit, you are not under the law" (Gal 5:18). This verse of scripture clearly states that if the Spirit of God leads you to do something, you are not under the law if you do that thing even if that thing is a commandment of the law. Sometimes, the Holy Spirit can lead one to perform a particular act or carry out a specific assignment. That does not mean that God is commanding everyone to do likewise. The Holy Spirit can lead you to give any amount of money or any portion of your income to the house of God, any house of God, or a particular minister, or a particular individual. This could be a tenth of your income. Now if you are led by the Spirit of God to give a tenth of your income at any time, then, do so, for as many as are led by the Spirit of God, these are sons of God (Rom 8:14). You are the child of your father: God. Obey your father's Spirit. He will also tell you where to give that specific offering.

This instruction to give a tenth of your income could be for a specific time or for life. Such instructions are specific and the fact that God instructed you specifically to give a tenth of your income does not mean that he commands the entire church on a doctrine of tithing. There have been many things that the Spirit had instructed Christians to do either as individuals or as a congregation which they did not make a doctrine. Tithing should not be elevated to the level of a generally binding doctrine just because God instructed some specific individuals to give a tenth of their incomes. When the Spirit leads a congregation to teach the truth about tithing and believers are allowed to commit themselves to tithing, then it will no longer be by law or compulsion, but as the Spirit leads individual believers. Such church is not tithing as under the law but as the Spirit leads.

SPECIFIC CONSECRATION OR COVENANT

Another reason for which a Christian may give a tenth of his income is if he specifically vowed to the Lord that he would give a tenth of his income to God's house. That is an individual or personal consecration. That is between him and God and has nothing do with other people. Whatever your right-hand does, let not your left hand know. Psalm 50 enjoins believers to fulfill their vows. If you made a vow to the Lord, then fulfill it. You bound yourself with a vow like Jacob, so you have to keep your promise to the Lord. God never asked Jacob to bring any tithe but Jacob volunteered a tenth of all that the Lord would give him.

God has not asked Christians for a tenth of their incomes. But if you volunteered it, it is binding on you, and you alone. For example, one may give tithe not because one agrees with popular teaching that one robs God and is cursed if one did not pay the tithe. In this case, one gives tithe as a freewill offering. Likewise, one may decide to give the first income earned in any job as a firstfruit. That is one's personal decision. Someone else may decide to give a firstfruit of first income from a new job, or first income from a new promotion and the like. That is their decision. Such a decision should not be binding on other believers. This is one perspective to what the Lord meant by our righteousness exceeding the righteousness of the Pharisees.

If you're a married woman, and bound yourself with such a voluntary tithing, discuss with your husband and get his permission to continue tithing. If he permits you then go on tithing but if he refuses to permit you, you have to respect his verdict (Num 30:6–8, Eph 5:22).

SOLEMN CONGREGATIONAL COMMITMENT

Another reason why you can give a tenth of your income is if your church decrees it. The Bible says that whatever the church permits on earth is permitted in heaven (Matt 16:19). A local church can decree that its members should give a tenth of their incomes. Thus, if you belong to a church that tithes, you are bound by that commitment to bring in your tithe as and when due. This is a collective commitment. However, in doing this the members of that church should be made to understand that what they are being asked to do is not a command of God or a doctrine rooted in the scriptures, but a practice instituted for administrative exigency. Also the use to which such tithe will be put must be made clear to the congregation. It must also be made clear to the congregation that failure to bring in such tithe does not damn the soul of a believer.

In conclusion, tithing is not a necessary or even an essential part of Christian worship. Similarly, New Testament believers are not required to tithe as a necessary source of revenue for the execution of the projects of the work of God. However, if tithe is paid or collected in the church, it should be with perfect knowledge and understanding of the nature and use of the tithe. Denominations that tithe should explain to their congregants why they tithe. Having done this, they will be within the scriptures when they collect tithes. Individuals that wish to tithe may not be hindered provided that they recognize that by giving tithes their prospects of making it to heaven is not bettered and that those who do not tithe are not worse off before God, neither are they "robbing" God. Those who tithe also have to do so provided that they do so out of free will, or they are led by the Spirit to do so, or there is a collective congregational agreement to do so.

Whatever we bring to the church is a freewill offering. Whether we bring a tenth, or less or more of our income does not impress God. What impresses God with our giving is not the quantity but the quality, not the amount but the mind. Galatians 6:7–8 warns:

> Do not be deceived, God is not mocked; for whatever a man sows, that he will also reap. For he who sows to his flesh will reap corruption, but he who sows to the Spirit will of the Spirit reap everlasting life.

If you, a child of God, sow in the hope and with the desire to be blessed in material things only and you pay tithes to gain material blessings, then you will also reap corruptible material things because you are sowing to the flesh. On the other hand, when you give by the leading of the Spirit or by your free will, out of love for God, then you will reap eternal reward because you are sowing to the Spirit. While we avoid sowing to the flesh, we must endeavor to share God's blessings with the servants of God who minister to us. The scriptures enjoin the believers thus:

> Let him who is taught the word share in all good things with him who teaches.
> And let us not grow weary while doing good, for in due season we shall reap if we do not lose heart. Therefore, as we have opportunity, let us do good to all, especially to those who are of the household of faith (Gal 6:6, 9–10).

This was the practice in the early church. They shared all things in common, they utilized every opportunity they had to do good to all, not only, but especially to those of the household of faith. This had nothing to do with tithe, but freewill giving and offerings. However, those who wish to give tithes are very free to do so in spirit—that is, as the Spirit leads, and truth—that is, right knowledge of God's word.

If you tithe, do it as unto the Lord, keep it to yourself. If you do not tithe, it is unto the lord you do not tithe, keep it to yourself. Let us not bring one another into judgment, or trouble the body of Christ for an issue that has no eternal or soul damning consequences. The scripture enjoins us that:

> It is good neither to . . . do anything by which your brother stumbles or is offended or is made weak. Do you have faith? Have it to yourself before God. Happy is he who does not condemn himself in what he approves. But he who doubts is condemned . . . because he does not . . . from faith; for whatever is not from faith is sin (Rom 14:21–23).

May the Lord bless you as you apply your mind to this, and decide on your own whether to tithe or not to tithe. Remember that the giving that God loves is that done willingly, freely, liberally, joyfully, cheerfully, zealously, generously, sacrificially, according to ability and as you purpose in your heart.

Chapter 10

THE CALL TO CALVARY
The "Tithe" that God Commands

GIVING TO THE HOUSE of God is very important but giving to God is even more important. God desires that we give to him first, then to his house. So what does God want us to give to him first? He tells us that in very clear language, "My son, give me your heart, and let your eyes observe my ways (Prov 23:26). Ever before you begin to observe God's way of giving, that is, to give the way God gives or to give how he wants you to give, he demands that you first give him your heart. Giving to the house of God has both eternal rewards as well as temporal material blessings attached to them. However, if one did not give one's heart to God, one will lose the eternal rewards even though one might gain the earthly material benefits. Two examples, one from the Old Testament and another from the New Testament, will buttress this.

In the Old Testament, Abraham started setting up altars and sacrificing to God only after he answered the call of God. When God called Abraham, he was not interested in Abraham's offering of his material possessions rather he wanted a father-and-son relationship with Abraham which started the moment Abraham obeyed his call to leave his father's house to a place that would be host to God's house:

> Now the LORD had said to Abram: "Get out of your country, from your family and from your father's house, to a land that I will show you . . ." So Abram departed as the LORD had spoken to him . . . And he moved from there to the mountain east of Bethel, and he pitched his tent with Bethel on the west and Ai on the east; there he built an altar to the LORD and called on the name of the LORD (Gen 12:1, 4, 8).

Thus, Abraham doing the work of God such as building altars had a meaning only after he had answered the call of God. The importance that God attaches to one giving one's heart to him is further stressed in the encounter of Cornelius in the New Testament.

Cornelius started by doing good works before answering the call of God. He was a just man who feared God and loved the nation of the Jews. His alms and righteous deeds were recognized in the sight of God, but that would not buy him salvation. He had to be corrected that he needed Jesus Christ. The apostle Peter was sent to him to preach Christ to him:

> So Cornelius said, "Four days ago I was fasting until this hour; and at the ninth hour I prayed in my house, and behold, a man stood before me in bright clothing, and said, 'Cornelius, your prayer has been heard, and your alms are remembered in the sight of God. Send therefore to Joppa and call Simon here, whose surname is Peter . . . When he comes, he will speak to you (Acts 10:30–32).

The scriptures record thus:

> Then Peter opened his mouth and said . . . The word which God sent to the children of Israel, preaching peace through Jesus Christ—He is Lord of all . . . And He commanded us to preach to the people, and to testify that it is He who was ordained by God to be Judge of the living and the dead. To Him all the prophets witness that, through His name, whoever believes in Him will receive remission of sins (Acts 10:34, 36, 42, 43).

Without accepting the gospel of Jesus Christ, one cannot have peace with God and one's good work and giving to the house of God will amount to no more than earthly alms to be remembered in sight of God but which cannot earn one eternal life. God wants you to have eternal life first before eternal rewards. Eternal life is in Christ only. You receive eternal life by grace when you give him your heart (Prov 23:26). Thereafter by the same grace you may render your services to God and give to his house.

Would you like to receive eternal life now? Then, give your heart to God by inviting Jesus Christ into your heart. Confess your sins to God, ask him to forgive, and ask Jesus to come into your heart. If you do that with all sincerity and honesty, you will receive eternal life in Christ.

BIBLIOGRAPHY

Cardoso, Renato. *The Right Way to Tithe.* Third Edition. Johannesburg: Universal Church of Kingdom of God (UCKG), 2004.

Constable, Giles. *Monastic Tithes: From their Origins to the Twelfth Century.* Cambridge: Cambridge University Press, 1964.

Dake, Finis J. *Dake's Annotated Reference Bible.* Georgia: Dake Bible Sales Inc., 1990.

Fanning, William. "Tithes." In *The Catholic Encyclopedia.* Vol. 14. New York: Robert Appleton, 1912. Retrieved from New Advent: http://www.newadvent.org/cathen/14741b.htm

McIntosh, Colin, ed. *Cambridge Advanced Learner's Dictionary.* 4th ed. Cambridge: Cambridge University Press, 2013.

Pick, Clive. *The Revelation of Financial Renewal.* Chichester: New Wine, 1998.

UCKG, HelpCenter. *Tithe The Firstfruits.* Finsbury Park: UCKG, 2013.

Weisberg, Jonathan. "A Jewish Perspective On Poverty: An Interview with Jonathan Weisberg." *WAJIBU* 12 (1995) 19–21.

www.ingramcontent.com/pod-product-compliance
Lightning Source LLC
Chambersburg PA
CBHW071051090426
42737CB00013B/2323

* 9 7 8 1 6 6 6 7 9 3 3 1 4 *